Releasing Your
Potential

by Myles Munroe

Take note that the name satan and related names are not capitalized. We choose not to acknowedge him, even to the point of violating grammatical rules.

Destiny Image Publishers
P.O. Box 310
Shippensburg, PA 17257-0310

"Speaking to the Purposes of God for this Generation"

ISBN 1-56043-072-9

For Worldwide Distribution
Printed in the U.S.A.

First Printing: 1992
Second Printing: 1992
Third Printing: 1992
Fourth Printing: 1993

Contents

Dedication

To my darling wife, Ruth, who is the essence of love, a personal source of encouragement and inspiration, and a cause for my passionate commitment for releasing my full potential;

To my daughter and son, Charisa and Chairo (Myles Jr.) for whose potential I live to see released and maximized;

To the millions of other children who were victims of abortion, robbed of the opportunity to release and maximize their awesome potential;

To the millions of great men and women who presently occupy the womb of some mother, children destined to change the world;

And to the millions of Third World people, around the world, whose potentials were oppressed and suppressed by the opinions and judgments of others.

Acknowledgments

This work is a synergistic product of many minds. I am forever grateful to the inspiration and wisdom of the many great men and women who, through their commitment to the passion for releasing their potential, have left a legacy to motivate me and my generation.

I am also grateful for the members, friends and colleagues at Bahamas Faith Ministries International, whose faithful prayers, patience and loyalty inspire me and allow me to fulfill my purpose and potential, especially my faithful executive administrator and eldest sister, Sheila Francis.

For the development and production of this book, I feel a deep sense of gratitude to:

—my wonderful wife, Ruth, and our children, for their patience, understanding and support during my many travels and involvements outside the home. You make it easy to fulfill God's will.

—the close circle of friends, pastors and board members— Richard Pinder (my friend and in-law indeed), Henry Francis, Dave Burrows, Wesley Smith and Jay Mullings (the gentle giant whose companionship on the road for many years of travel has contributed to the releasing of my potential)—whose loyalty and commitment to the vision can take credit for most of what God has done in my life.

—Kathy Miller, my gifted and diligent transcriber, editor and advisor, who again labored in childbirth with me and this project. And once again to Marsha Blessing of Destiny Image, who patiently pursued me in my busy travel schedule to meet the deadlines.

—the best friends in the ministry anyone could ever have: Ternel Nelson, Bertril Baird, Peter Morgan, Fuschia

Pickett, Ezekiel Guti, Fred Price, Allen Langstaff, Jerry Horner and Kingsley Fletcher.

—and finally, to the Source and Supplier of all potential, the Omni-potent One, the Father and Lord of all creation, and His Son, my elder Brother, Jesus Christ, and my personal Counselor, the Holy Spirit. Thanks for the privilege of serving You.

Foreword

Solomon wrote in the book of Ecclesiastes:

Let us hear the conclusion of the whole matter: Fear God, and keep His commandments: for this is the whole duty of man (Ecclesiastes 12:13 KJV).

We know that in this context the word *fear* does not mean "to be afraid of" but rather "to have reverence for" or "to revere". This is man's duty: to have reverence for God and to keep (do) His commandments. But the word *duty* has been grossly neglected.

When we hear the word *commandment*, we ultimately think of morality: Thou shalt not kill; neither shalt thou commit adultery; neither shalt thou steal; neither shalt thou bear false witness against thy neighbor, etc. We seldom think about God's commandment (not a suggestion) found in the first chapter of Genesis where the Creator said to man, His greatest achievement:

Be *fruitful*, and multiply, and replenish the earth, and subdue it: and have dominion over the fish of the sea, and over the fowl of the air, and over every living thing that moveth upon the earth (Genesis 1:28 KJV).

God's purpose for giving man life is contained in these verses. Over the years that purpose has been neglected. Therefore, I call this the "forgotten" commandment.

Myles Munroe addresses this forgotten commandment in this insightful study on purpose and potential. Like a skilled surgeon, with knife in hand, he dissects and delineates man's need to discover his potential and his purpose for being here. By the anointing of the Holy Spirit, Myles also challenges us to discover and activate our purpose and potential.

There is a saying that goes something like this: "The mind is a terrible thing to waste." That, without question, is true, but I think wasted purpose and potential are even more tragic than that. If you have ever questioned: "Why am I here?" "Why was I born?" "What is life all about, anyway?" then this book is *must* reading for you.

Or perhaps you have been groping in the darkness of life, trying to discover your purpose for being. If this is true, I highly recommend this book. Read it, meditate on it, dissect it and digest it. Your effort to understand and act on the teaching in this book will make a dramatic difference in your life. Then the world will be a better place because you lived to find your *purpose* and *potential*.

Dr. Frederick K.C. Price
Crenshaw Christian Center
Los Angeles, California

Preface

The poorest man in the world is the man without a dream. The most frustrated man in the world is the man with a dream that never becomes reality. I am certain that every individual on this planet—no matter which race, culture, nationality or socio-economic status—has had a dream of some sort. The ability of children to dream is a natural instinct instilled by the Creator. No matter how poor or rich we are, whether we were born in the bush village of an underdeveloped nation or amidst the marble floors of the aristocracy of society, we all have childhood dreams. These dreams are visual manifestations of our purpose, seeds of destiny planted in the soil of our imagination. I am convinced that God created and gave us the gift of imagination to provide us with a glimpse of our purpose in life and to activate the hidden ability within each of us. Purpose is the reason why something was made. It is the end for which the means exist. It is the source of the dream and the vision you carried in your heart from childhood. It is the key to your fulfillment.

It is a fact that every manufacturer makes a product to fulfill a specific purpose, and every product is designed with the ability to fulfill this purpose. In essence, the *potential* of a product is determined by its purpose. This is true of everything God created, including you. The purpose of a seed is to reproduce trees. Therefore, by God's design, they possess the ability or potential to fulfill this purpose. But because a seed has the *potential* to produce a forest, does not mean it will. One of the greatest tragedies in nature is the destruction of a seed or the isolation of a seed from the soil. Consequently, the death of a seed is the burial of a forest. Having ability is good, but keeping ability is bad.

Your life has the potential to fulfill your purpose. If, however, you imprison that potential, you rob your life of its purpose and fulfillment. You and every other individual on this planet possess an awesome treasure. Too much of this treasure is buried every day, untapped and untouched, in the cemeteries of our world. Much talent, skill and creativity have been lost to the world for want of a little courage. Many obscure men and women enter eternity pregnant with potential, with a still-born purpose. Living with ability brings responsibility. Dying with ability reveals irresponsibility.

Everything in creation was designed to function on the simple principle of *receiving* and *releasing*. Life depends on this principle. What if the plants refused to *release* the oxygen they possess or if we human beings refused to *release* the carbon dioxide we produce? The result would be chaos and death for the entire planet. Unreleased potential is not only useless, it is dangerous—both for the person or thing who failed to release it and for everything that lives with them. Dormant potential is not healthy, advantageous, safe or effective. You must understand that your valuable deposit of potential was given to enrich the lives of others. When potential is kept, it self-destructs.

The tremendous potential you and I have been given is locked inside us, waiting for demands to be made on it. We have a responsibility to use what God stored in us for the good of the world. We dare not leave this planet with it. Many of us are aware of the ability we have inside, but we have been frustrated by our failure to release this ability. Some of us blame our historical circumstances. Others blame social status. Still others transfer the responsibility for their failure and frustration to their lack of formal education or their less than ideal opportunities.

Over the years, I have come to realize that no excuse can be given to justify the destruction of the seed of potential that God placed within you. You *can* become the man or woman you were born to be. You *can* accomplish the vision you saw. You *can* build that business you planned. You *can* develop that school you imagine. *You* are the only one who can stop you. No matter what your environment, you have the ability to change your attitude and your internal environment until they are conducive to the germination of your potential seed. The purpose of this material is to help you understand and appropriate the principles necessary for *Releasing Your Potential*. You must not add to the wealth of the graveyard. You owe it to the next generation to live courageously so the treasure of your potential is unleashed. The world needs what God deposited in you for the benefit of your contemporaries and all the generations to follow.

Tap the untapped. Release the reservoir.

Introduction

It was a cool, wet, rainy September Sunday afternoon in the historic city of London. We had just finished a delightful meal when our host suggested that we take a quiet stroll through the neighborhood park. I had been traveling for eight days, keeping a schedule that had to that point taxed me both mentally and physically, so it was a rare pleasure and a welcomed joy to embrace the opportunity to spend those quiet moments alone.

We entered the well-manicured grounds and observed with a degree of surprise the number of people who had the same idea. My host took delight in pointing out to me the various plants, birds, flowers and lush vegetation. After we had walked a short distance, we were interrupted by an elderly gentleman who greeted my host with great joy. My host introduced me, then continued his conversation with the gentleman. I took the opportunity to steal away for that private, relaxing walk I had desired. After I had walked for a few minutes, the pathway meandered to the entrance of an old cemetery. My tenacious interest in history drew me to explore the historical nature of the tombstones and the grave markers just to satisfy my curiosity. What an awesome experience it was to read and study the many names, dates and quotes as these silent stones spoke. Names like John Hill 1800-1864, Elizabeth Robinson 1790-1830, and so on gave evidence of the years of British history buried there.

Then I came upon a small grave, perhaps three feet in length, that read, "Markus Rogers, 1906-1910." Written below the name was the quote, "Gone but not forgotten." A brief calculation revealed that this was the resting place of a four-year-old child. After scanning the hundreds of markers and stones, my eyes rested, once again, upon the grave of this child. Deep contemplation settled upon me. I noticed that almost all the tombstones, including the child's, had the words "Rest in Peace" inscribed on them. Many questions and thoughts raced through my mind: *Who were the child's parents? What was the cause of death? What was his purpose in being born? What special natural talents and gifts did he possess that were never displayed and never benefited anyone? What inventions or discoveries could he have shared with the human race? How many great works of art, books or songs died in this precious infant?*

As silence answered, I suddenly applied the questions to the many tombstones that surrounded this child's resting place. Some of the others had recorded life spans of thirty, forty, sixty and even seventy-five years. Yet the only testimony to their time on this planet was "Rest In Peace." Then I wondered: *How can you rest in peace if you died with all your potential inside?* As the wet, misty rain formed dew drops on my cheeks, I walked away thinking: *What a tragedy it is for a child to die at such a tender age, before he has the opportunity to realize his full potential.*

Immediately a quiet voice screamed in my head: *Is it not a greater tragedy if those who lived to old age also carried their books, art, music, inventions, dreams and potential to the grave?* Suddenly the rain seemed to turn to sweat as I pondered the awesome implications of this question. One of my greatest fears is that many who still walk the streets of our world, perhaps some who are reading this book, will also deposit in the cemeteries of their communities the wealth of potential locked inside them. I trust that you will not allow the grave to rob this world of your latent, awesome *potential*.

There are five billion people on this planet. Each one is very special, unique, original and significant. All possess a genetic combination that codes them as distinct individuals whose fingerprints cannot be duplicated. There is no one like you now, nor will there ever be another. Each of us—whether black, brown, yellow, red or white—was conceived by destiny, produced by purpose and packaged with potential to live a meaningful, fulfilling life. Deep within you lies a seed of greatness waiting to be germinated. You have been endued with natural talents, gifts, desires and dreams. All humanity, in all cultures, races and socio-economic situations, lives with the natural instinct to manifest this potential.

The entire creation possesses this principle of potential. Everything has the natural instinct to release its ability. The plant and animal kingdom abounds with evidences of this fact. The Creator designed everything with this principle of potential, which can be simplified to the concept of a seed. The biblical document states that God created everything with "seed in it according to their kinds" (Genesis 1:12). In essence, hidden within everything is the potential to fulfill itself and produce much more than we see.

Please note that when God created the earth and placed man in the garden, He did not give man a finished product. Although God knew that man would need food, clothes, shelter, transportation and other elements of comfort, He did not make all these things instantly available. God commanded the man: "Be fruitful, and increase in number; fill the earth and subdue it" (Genesis 1:28). Each of these commands is based on the assumption that the *ability* to be fruitful and the *potential* to multiply and replenish and subdue were present in the man, waiting to be activated, tapped and released. This command also implies that fruitfulness (release of hidden life) and multiplication (reproduction of hidden life) are not dependent on God but on the individual who possesses the seed.

You have the ability to accomplish everything your God-given purpose demands. Your Creator has given you the responsibility of releasing this precious seed in obedience to His commands. The releasing of your potential is not up to God but you.

Henry Ford once said, "My best friend is the one who brings out the best in me." It is my hope that this book becomes one of your best friends as it inspires you to strive to release your hidden abilities for the benefit of the world around you and for your personal fulfillment.

For the last two decades, I have devoted myself to understanding, activating, tapping and releasing my potential and the potential of others. An integral part of this devotion was the study and observation of the lives of some of this world's leading men and women—people who have affected their societies positively because they released and maximized their potential. As a result, I am convinced that every individual comes into this world with a deposit of potential that far exceeds any attempt to measure its potency. I also believe that this potential is viable in spite of the external environment in which it exists. My studies and experience have also revealed that this potential must be released by applying specific principles that are evident in every case in the lives of those people who tapped the deposit God placed within them. The presence and application of these principles was visible no matter what ethnic, social, academic or economic situation prevailed.

Although I have said that everyone possesses great potential and the capacity to release this awesome ability, I also believe, with great sadness, that not everyone will become all the Creator intended them to be. Too many people are mere products of their environment, allowing themselves to be victimized by the opinions of others and the assessments of human analysis. They lack the will to change or challenge the limitations placed upon them by themselves and others, and thus fail to take the necessary steps to develop their potential.

I also believe, however, that anyone, of any age, and in any circumstances, can transform himself if he wants to. You *can* become all God designed you to be if you are willing to defy the norm and dare to believe God's assessment of your ability. It's not what you don't know that hurts you. It's what you know that just ain't so.

The purpose of this book is to make you examine and challenge the many opinions you have lived under for years. My deepest desire is to release in you the courage to pursue the depth of ability that lies deep within you, to tap the reserve of life yet unseen by your peers, and to provoke you to unbridle the silent wealth of power that is screaming for exposure. After you've finished reading this book, read it again until the principles and the truths it contains become a natural part of your thinking and you come to the awareness that understanding and releasing your potential is simply *becoming yourself* as God our Creator originally intended. Nothing is impossible to him who believes.

**A seed, until it is released,
is only a promise of a tree.**

1 | The Tragedy of Unreleased Potential

The death of a seed is the burial of a forest.

The voice over the intercom announcing that we had finally begun our descent after ten hours of flying startled me from my restless sleep. With a deep sense of anticipation, I gathered my thoughts and prepared for landing. It was my first trip to the great South American country of Brazil. Because I had been invited to address a conference of ten thousand leaders and laymen, I felt an awesome responsibility upon me. My time in this country of beautiful and complex cultures and ethnic heritages would be a lesson in humanity's oneness. It confirmed once again that despite our minor differences, we are all the same.

Seven days into my stay, my host and translator took me on a tour of their beautiful capital, Brasilia. After visiting the well-organized city and government buildings and touring the stately monuments of the picturesque city, we entered one of my favorite places to visit—the national museum. Being an artist and a lover of history, I enjoy these excursions in every country I visit.

This day in Brasilia was no exception. I felt great appreciation for the beautiful and important works of art around me. As I viewed, studied and admired the tremendous historical pieces and the priceless testimonies of the glory of this nation's past and present, I was once again reminded that each painting, sculpture and specimen was the product of the release of someone's potential. Although many of the artists are dead, their works are not. Display after display gave evidence to potential that had not been buried with the artists. Because they had dared to expose the talent hidden within them, I and many others were enjoying, appreciating and being inspired by their imaginative works.

Throughout time, the great and small works of individuals—be they paintings, books, music, poetry, drama, architecture, inventions or the development of theories—have affected the lives of many. All who have helped to shape our society's destiny—the giants who teach us and inspire us—used their potential with a passion and refused to let circumstances dictate their future. The museum in Brazil, like all the museums of the world, is a constant reminder that someone lived who refused to let death have the final word on their potential. *Their released potential is the world's inheritance.*

I believe earth itself is a museum. Each of us comes into this world with an assignment to fulfill. God commissions us to leave for the following generations something from which they can learn and be inspired. The abilities to complete these assignments lie within us. The tools are our natural talents, gifts and ambitions.

Each of us comes into this world with an assignment to fulfill.

Unless you accept the responsibility for activating your abilities, the next generation will enter the museum of life and notice a vacant space in earth's displays. The sign below the placed reserved to display the fruit of your potential will read: "Assignment unfinished. Potential unreleased."

The Abortion of Ability

"The price of greatness is responsibility." These words were spoken by Sir Winston Churchill. They contain a truth that should be guarded and heeded. The graveyards are full of great men and women who never became great because they did not give their ability responsibility. This untapped ability is called potential. Each of us comes into the world pregnant with unlimited potential. We are capable of much more than we have already done. Unless we expose, during the course of our lives, all that God placed within us for the good of mankind, our potential will be aborted.

The graveyards are full of great men and women who never became great because they did not give their ability responsibility.

Abortion is one of today's most controversial issues. It is polarizing many communities. It has also become a hot political issue in many countries where it is used to manipulate the reins of power. Many people think of this concern as a recent one. Although it is causing much stir in our societies, the concern over abortion is not new. The truth is that the abortion issue is as old as time. The fact of abortion is as old as man.

Abortion is not limited to the physical termination of a fetus in a mother's womb. The first act of abortion was performed in the Garden of Eden when the first man, Adam, was given the responsibility for carrying the entire human race within his loins. In Adam was the seed of all generations and the strength of all mankind. God's instructions to Adam were very simple and clear:

> **You are free to eat from every tree in the garden; but you must not eat from the tree of the knowledge of good and evil, for when you eat of it you will surely die** (Genesis 2:16-17).

To *surely die* means to definitely cease from manifesting the fruitfulness that exists within a thing. Death, in its simplest form, is the termination of potential. To abort means to terminate life before its full potential has or can be realized, before the person, animal, plant, etc. is given an opportunity to fulfill its full potential.

**Death, in its simplest form,
is the termination of potential.**

God created everything with the hidden ability to fulfill itself. The Bible's record of creation states that the seed of everything is in itself to produce after its kind (Genesis 1:12). All creation possesses the hidden ability to be everything it is suppose to be:

In every seed there is a forest,
in every fish, a school,
in every bird, a flock,
in every cow, a herd,
in every girl, a woman,
in every boy, a man, and
in every man, a nation.

It is important for us to remember that *every great tree was once a seed, every woman was once a fetus, every man was once a boy, and every nation was once in the loins of a man.* It is also interesting to note that whenever God deals with man, He always speaks in terms of the generational seed within his loins. In God's calculation of life, one equals many, little equals much, small equals great, and less equals more. Therefore, to abort a seed is to kill a forest, to abort a cow is to kill a herd, to abort a boy is to kill a man, to abort a girl is to kill a woman, and to abort a man is to destroy a nation. God told Abraham, the great patriarch of history,

> **I will make you a great nation and I will bless you; I will make your name great and you will be a blessing. ...and all peoples on earth will be blessed through you** (Genesis 12:2-3).

Abortion is the ultimate tragedy. It robs life of its essence and denies the future its value.

Abortion Through Ignorance

Abortion is the ignorance of responsibility and the denial of obligation. Abortion is self-comfort at the expense of fruitfulness, because *all abortions sacrifice responsibility. The abortion of potential condemns the future.* This reality has caused the development of an entire discipline of science. Ecology and environmental studies, as these areas of concern are known, build their premises on the word *extinction*, meaning "the termination of the potential force within creation to fulfill itself."

Abortion is the ignorance of responsibility and the denial of obligation.

It is amazing that man, with all his attempts to minimize the abortion of various species in the animal and plant kingdom by investing billions of dollars to protect animals, plants, forests and the ozone layer, has neglected to prioritize the position of human beings in the scheme of things. While man fights to protect whales, owls, trees and fish, he also battles for the right to terminate human babies. Perhaps the situation would improve if every doctor who performs this tragic operation would be reminded before each abortion that the opportunity to perform this surgery is his only because his mother did not abort him.

The abortion issue is, therefore, not just a problem of the taking of a life, though that is the fatal end result. Even more, abortion is the ignorance and the lack of understanding of the principle of potential that pervades our world. The majority of those who die each year are guilty of abortion because they didn't understand the basic relevance of the concept of potential to their individual lives.

The abortion of potential is the death of the future. It affects generation after generation. When Adam broke God's law, he aborted his seed's potential for becoming all they were intended to be. Men and women throughout all ages have fallen far short of the glory of the Creator. The word *glory* means the "true nature" or "full essence" of a thing. In other words, *to fall short of glory means to live below your true potential.* This is what God calls sin. Sin is not a behavior; it is a disposition. One of the great biblical writers states it this way:

> **I consider that our present sufferings are not worth comparing with the glory that will be revealed in us. The creation waits in eager expectation for [the glory of] the sons of God to be revealed** (Romans 8:18-19).

This passage states that the fall of man prevented the full glory or true potential of mankind from being revealed or manifested. All creation was affected by man's sin. God's creation is waiting for man's glory or true potential to be exposed because creation's destiny is tied to man's. Thus, any abortion, whether it's the abortion of a dream, a vision, art, music, writing, business, leadership or inventions, affects both nature and the succeeding generations of man.

How many children yet unborn were destined to sing the song you have never written?

When Adam aborted the vision God had placed in his heart and disobeyed the directives of the Manufacturer, he changed the lives of the entire human race that lay hidden in his loins. The book of Romans states:

> **Therefore, just as sin entered the world through one man, and death through sin, and in this way death came to all men, because all sinned [in Adam]... Consequently, just as the result of one trespass was condemnation for all men, so also the result of one act of righteousness was justification that brings life for all men** (Romans 5:12,18).

It is vital that we understand the principle demonstrated in these passages. It is the awesome realization that if your potential is not released, it will affect this generation and all the generations of man yet to live. Even creation will testify against you. If you abort your potential, you will be guilty of robbing the world of the treasure you came to this planet to deliver. *The fact that you were born is evidence that God knew earth needed the potential you are pregnant with.* It is, therefore, imperative that you refuse to leave this planet without giving birth to those dreams, ideas, visions and inventions you carry in the womb of your faith right now. Do not abort your baby of potential. *Rob the grave of the treasure you carry.* Leave the picture of your potential on the wall of history in the museum of the earth.

PRINCIPLES

---

1. Your released potential is the world's inheritance.

2. You came into the world pregnant with unlimited potential.

3. You are capable of much more than you have already done.

4. Creation's destiny is tied to the release of your potential.

5. The fact that you were born is evidence that God knew earth needed the potential you are pregnant with.

2 | How Will You Be Remembered?

Knowledge of ability is the introduction of responsibility.

Come with me in your imagination to the funeral of a loved one. Picture yourself driving to the funeral parlor or the church, parking your car and getting out. As you walk inside the building, notice the flowers and the soft organ music. See the faces of friends and family as you move through the room. Feel the shared sorrow of losing and the joy of having known that radiates from the hearts of the people there.

As you walk to the front of the room and look inside the casket, you come face to face with yourself. This is your funeral, five years from today. All these people have come to honor you and to express feelings of love and appreciation for your life. As you take a seat and wait for the service to begin, look at the program in your hand. Five persons will speak. The first speaker is from your family, immediate and extended—your children, brothers, sisters, nephews, nieces, aunts, uncles, cousins and grandparents who have come from all over the country to attend. The second speaker is to be one of your friends, someone who can give a sense of what you were as a person. The third speaker is from your work or profession. The fourth speaker is from your church or some community organization where you were involved in service. The fifth and final speaker is your spouse.

Now think deeply. What would you like each of these speakers to say about you and your life? What kind of husband or wife, father or mother would you like their words to reflect? What kind of son or daughter or cousin? What kind of friend or working associate?

Before you read further, take a few minutes to seriously consider these questions. I firmly believe that the greatest tragedy in life is not death, but life...life that fails to fulfill its purpose and potential.

The greatest tragedy in life is not death, but life...life that fails to fulfill its purpose and potential.

Live Effectively

Through this book, you are being made aware of the great treasure you possess, which is your potential. I have addressed millions of people on this issue of living effectively. Repeatedly I have stressed that it is better to have never been born than to live and not fulfill the purpose for which you were given life. This truth is echoed in Ecclesiastes 6:3-6.

> A man may have a hundred children and live many years; yet no matter how long he lives, if he cannot enjoy his prosperity and does not receive proper burial, I say that a stillborn child is better off than he. It comes without meaning, it departs in darkness, and in darkness its name is shrouded. Though it never saw the sun or knew anything, it has more rest than does that man.

This passage asserts that it would be better for an individual never to have been born than for him to live on this planet many years and not fulfill the purpose for which God gave him birth. In essence, when you become aware of the tremendous potential that resides within you, you are obligated to release that wealth to the world around you.

Ability and Responsibility

What lies behind you is history and what lies before you is future, but these are both tiny matters compared to what lies within you. You may not be able to change your past, and your future is yet unlived, but the present provides you with opportunities to maximize your life and the ability that lives within you. You must take responsibility for your ability—no one else can do it for you.

You must take responsibility for your ability.

Are you living a stillbirth life? Are you aborting your entire purpose for living? I encourage you to take responsibility right now for your ability. Determine to activate, release and maximize your potential for the sake of the next generation. Leave your footprints in the sands of the history of your country. *Live fully so you can die effectively. Let your life write the speech of your death and give your potential to the family of man for the glory of God.* Remember "well done" is much better than "well said." Don't just talk about your potential dreams, visions and ideas. Step out now and determine to do them. Dare to believe that what you have already accomplished is but a minute percentage of what you *can* do. Move beyond the familiar patterns and experiences of your life to the dreams and plans and imaginations that wait within you to be fulfilled.

Will Your Abilities Be Lost to the World?

You possess awesome potential within waiting to be activated and released. The release of your potential demands that you refuse to be satisfied with your latest accomplishment. Only then will you tap into the vast bill of credit with which you were born. Because potential, by definition, is the large, unknown bank of resources you were given at birth, what you have accomplished is no longer your potential. Releasing your potential requires a willingness to move beyond the familiar into the realm of possibilities.

**The release of your potential demands
that you refuse to be satisfied
with your latest accomplishment.**

If you attempt new things and make choices that stretch your horizons, you will embark on an exciting journey. You will begin to see the marvelous being God created you to be—a being filled with more capabilities than you ever dreamed possible. The journey begins when you gain an understanding of what potential is and how you can release it. For once you understand the magnitude of the wealth God gave you, to turn from consciously and conscientiously unwrapping God's gift is to abort your potential and refuse to fulfill the purpose for which He gave you life. The knowledge of what you have failed to use to benefit yourself, your contemporaries and the generations to follow will judge you on the great day of accountability. Potential is given to be released, not wasted.

**Some men have thousands of reasons
why they cannot do what they want to,
when all they need is one reason why they can.**

PRINCIPLES

1. **God placed potential in you to benefit the world.**

2. **Potential is the large, unknown bank of resources you were given at birth.**

3. **Potential must be used or it will be aborted.**

4. **Satisfaction with success kills potential.**

3 | What Is Potential?

The abortion of potential is the death of the future.

Potential is...

...unexposed ability...reserved power...untapped strength...capped capabilities...unused success...dormant gifts...hidden talents...latent power.

...what you can do that you haven't yet done...where you can go that you haven't yet gone...who you can be that you haven't yet been...what you can imagine that you haven't yet imagined...how far you can reach that you haven't yet reached...what you can see that you haven't yet seen...what you can accomplish that you haven't yet accomplished.

Thus, potential is the sum of who you are that you have yet to reveal. It's a deposit that waits to be released and maximized. You are capable of much more than you are presently thinking, imagining, doing or being. That is your potential. Unless you continually try to reach higher, go farther, see over and grasp something greater than you now know, you will never discover your full potential.

**You are capable of much more
than you are presently
thinking, imagining, doing or being.**

The Potential Principle

Suppose we stood in a vast forest and I asked you to describe what you saw. You might say that you saw trees and plants and flowers and insects and birds and animals. But in truth that is not all you would be seeing. For within each of those things are the seeds for more trees, plants, flowers, insects, birds and animals. That's the potential principle. Your observation would be fact but not truth.

If, for example, I hold an apple seed in my hand, I hold much more than one seed. In every seed there is a tree, and in every tree there are apples with seeds in them. And the seeds contain more apple trees that contain fruit that contain seeds and so on. In fact I hold one apple seed. In truth I hold an entire orchard. That is potential—what yet can be.

Understanding Potential

God created everything with potential. Genesis 1:12 describes how God created the plants and the trees, each "bearing seed according to their kinds." The first chapter of Genesis also gives an account of the creation of the birds, the creatures of the sea, the livestock, the creatures that move along the ground and the wild animals. They too were given the ability to reproduce according to their kinds. Thus, every living thing that God created was blessed with potential. Each possessed the capability to be much more than they appeared to be at any one time. Each contained the seed from which future generations of plants, birds, fish and animals would come.

**Every living thing that God created
was blessed with potential.**

God also planted within you the ability to be much more than you are at any one moment. Like the apple seed, you possess hidden resources and capabilities. Most of the potential God gave you at birth still remains within you, unseen and unused. What I see when I meet you on any given day is not all you are.

The Source of All Potential

Everything that was and is was in God. Before God created anything, there was only God. Thus, God had within Him the potential for everything He made. Nothing exists that was not first in God. *God is the source of all life, because before anything was, God is.*

**Everything that was and is
was in God.**

"In the beginning God created the heavens and the earth" (Genesis 1:1). He pulled everything that He made out of Himself. Indeed, the beginning was in God before it began. God started start. If the book of Genesis had started with Genesis 1:0, it might have read, "Before there was a beginning, there was God. Before there was a creation, there was a Creator. Before anything was, there was God."

God did not begin when the beginning began. He was in the beginning before the beginning had a beginning. "In the beginning was the Word, and the Word was with God, and the Word was God" (John 1:1). Everything in the world we know was in God before it came to be seen. "Through [God] all things were made; without Him nothing was made that has been made" (John 1:3). Thus, God is the source of all potential. He is everything we haven't seen yet.

When we describe this characteristic of God, we say that He is omnipotent. *Omni* means "always" and *potent* means "full of power." God is always full of power. He can always do more than He has already done.

God's Creation Process

God's process in creating the world follows an interesting pattern. *First, God planned what He wanted to create. Second, He decided what kind of material substance He wanted His creation to be made from. Third, God spoke to the substance from which the thing was to be created and, fourth, exactly what He spoke came forth from that to which He spoke.*

Thus, when God wanted to make plants, He spoke to the ground, because that is the material substance from which He wanted them to come (Genesis 1:11). When He wanted to create animals, God again spoke to the ground because He had planned for animals to be made of dirt (Genesis 1:24). Fish came forth from the sea when God spoke to it (Genesis 1:20). The sun, the moon and the stars appeared in the expanse of the sky when God called them into being (Genesis 1:14-17). Everything came forth when God spoke to a material substance, in accordance with the plan He had developed before He spoke the world into being.

God Gave *You* Potential

When God created human beings, He spoke to Himself. You came forth from God because God planned that human beings should be spirit even as He is Spirit. Too many people never discover God's purpose for creating them. They look everywhere but to God for the meaning of their existence. Their lives are unfulfilled and their potential is wasted. God looks at them and bemoans their loss: "If you only knew who you are. If you only knew what you can do.

If you only knew why I gave you life." Perhaps that is God's attitude toward you.

Remember, few things are impossible when they are tackled with diligence and skill. Great works are performed not by strength, but by perseverance. God created you with potential. He waits to see what you will do with the remarkable gift He gave you.

PRINCIPLES

1. Potential is what yet can be.
2. God created everything with potential.
3. God is the Source of all potential.
4. What God planned came forth from the substance to which He spoke.
5. When God wanted you, He spoke to Himself.

4 | How to Release Your Potential

Rob the grave of the potential you carry within. Release your potential.

By now you must understand what potential is and the tremendous responsibility you have to release your potential. In this chapter I want to give you six basic principles that are fundamental to *all* potential, as well as ten requirements that are keys to the effective use of *your* potential.

Principles That Govern Potential

Before you can begin to grasp the nature and the magnitude of your potential, you must understand the laws that control all potential. God set these laws when He tapped His creative abilities to make visible that which existed but was invisible. The first two chapters of the Bible tell the story of this unleashing of God's potential.

Principle #1—What God speaks to is the source for what He creates.

An examination of the process God used to create the world reveals that everything God created was brought forth by His spoken word. Whatever God spoke to became the source for the creation God planned to bring forth. When

God wanted plants, He spoke to the dirt (Genesis 1:11-12). When God wanted animals, He spoke to the ground (Genesis 1:24-25). When God wanted fish, He spoke to the waters (Genesis 1:20-21). When God wanted stars, He spoke to the gases in the heavens (Genesis 1:14-15). Throughout creation, whatever God spoke to became the source from which the created thing came, and exactly what God spoke came forth from the substance to which He spoke.

Principle #2—All things have the same components and essence as the sources from which they came.

The source to which God spoke during the creative process also becomes the final home of all He has created. When God's creations die, they return to the source from which He took them. Thus, plants came from the dirt and return to the dirt. Animals also came from and return to the ground. Fish came from and return to the sea, and stars came from and return to the gases of the heavens. This is possible because all things are made of the same stuff from which they came. If we take apart a plant or an animal and look at its cells beneath a microscope, we discover that plants and animals are one hundred percent dirt. They are composed of dirt because they came from dirt.

Principle #3—All things must be maintained by the sources from which they came.

God's world also reveals that whatever God creates must be sustained and maintained by the source from which it came. Plants that are pulled from the ground die. Animals that cease to eat plants or other animals die. Fish that are removed from water die. Flowers that are cut for arrangements wilt sooner than those that remain attached to the plant. Indeed, all living things die the instant they are removed from their sources. The signs of death and decay may not be immediately evident, but nonetheless, they are dead. None of God's living creations can survive without the resources and the nourishment provided by the substances from which they came.

Principle #4—The potential of all things is related to the sources from which they came.

Because all things are composed of the sources from which they came, they also contain as little or as much potential as their original substances. Animals have no greater or lesser potential than the dirt from which they came. Plants also have only the potential of the dirt. If the soil is lacking in nutrients or the ability to hold water, the plants attached to that soil are going to be adversely affected by the poor quality of the soil. Likewise, the animals that eat the plants that are growing in the unhealthy soil are going to receive less nutrients than if they had eaten plants that were growing in healthy soil.

No product can be more powerful than the source from which it came. A wooden table, for example, is only as strong as the wood of the tree from which the furniture maker built it. If you make a table from a rotten tree, you'll have a rotten table. A floor made of pine will not withstand wear as well as a floor made of oak, because pine is a softer wood than oak. The characteristics of the tree from which the flooring boards were made always affect the quality of the finished floor.

No product can be more powerful than the source from which it came.

Thus, the quality of any product is dependent upon the quality of the components used in the product, which is dependent upon the quality of the materials used in the components. *The potential of something is always related to the potential of the source from which it came.* Nothing can be greater than its source.

Principle #5—Everything in life has the potential to fulfill its purpose.

The purpose of a thing is the original intent or desire of the one who created it. Thus, the purpose of a thing cannot be known by asking anyone other than the designer or the manufacturer. If we entered the laboratory of an inventor and you asked me what a certain contraption was supposed to do, I might guess at what service or function it could perform, but only the inventor would be able to confirm or reject my suggestion.

The purpose of a thing cannot be known by asking anyone other than the designer or the manufacturer.

Likewise, *the ability of that product to fulfill its purpose is designed into the product.* No manufacturer would suggest that you use his appliance to wash clothes unless he intended for it to wash clothes. If I assume that the machine is a clothes dryer and complain to the dealer that the machine won't dry my clothes, the manufacturer will most certainly respond, "But that machine isn't supposed to dry clothes. Use it to wash clothes and it'll work fine. But don't ask it to dry clothes, because it can't. I didn't build it to dry clothes." The manufacturer determines both the product's purpose and how it will function to fulfill that purpose.

Principle #6—Potential is determined and revealed by the demands placed on it by its creator.

What a product can potentially do is determined by what the manufacturer of the product asks it to do. Potential is revealed by the faith of the manufacturer in his product and the expectations he places upon it. If a manufacturer of small trucks designs them to carry one-half ton, the company will not advertise their product as having the ability to carry one ton. Why? Because the manufacturer knows that he cannot require the truck to carry a full ton when the specifications under which it was built designate that the maximum capacity is one-half ton.

**Potential is revealed by
the faith of the manufacturer in his product
and the expectations he places upon it.**

The manufacturer will not ask the product to perform more or less than he designed it to do. If a manufacturer requires a product to do something, you can be sure that he believes the ability to perform the task was built into the product.

Keys to Releasing Your Potential

Building potential into a product does not necessarily mean that potential will be revealed. Many of us have appliances in our homes that are capable of much more than we require of them. Perhaps you use your oven to bake but not broil because you don't know how to use the broiler. Or maybe you have a vacuum cleaner that has the ability to clean up water as well as dirt, but you haven't used that feature because you aren't aware that the manufacturer built that capability into the machine.

God has built many abilities into men and women. Too often, however, we fail to use that potential because we don't understand either the magnitude of our capabilities or the requirements that are necessary to unleash our power. The following are keys to the effective release of the wealth of your potential.

Key #1—You must know your Source.

Every product you purchase includes a certain degree of guarantee based on a relationship with the one from whom you bought the product. Thus, if you want to buy a car, you will first research the integrity of the various car manufacturers and the quality of their cars. Then you will look for an authorized dealer in your area who will explain and follow the manufacturer's specifications.

God is your manufacturer. If you want to know your potential, you must go to Him. God, through His authorized dealer, the Holy Spirit, is the only One who can reveal to you the qualities and characteristics of your potential and the precautions you must heed to avoid wasting or abusing your abilities. Unless you get to know your Source and establish a relationship with Him through His Son, Jesus Christ, you have no hope of releasing your potential. Knowing God is the foundational key upon which all the other keys rest.

Key #2—You must understand how you were designed to function.

Every manufacturer designs his product with certain features and specifications. Then he gives you an instruction book that clarifies the definitions of the features so you can become familiar with both the parts of the equipment and their functions. Thus, a car manufacturer describes in the manual how the engine, the brakes, the windshield wipers, etc. are supposed to operate, because he knows that you will not get optimum performance from the car unless you understand how the various parts of the car were intended to work.

God designed you with intricate features and capabilities. If you fail to learn from God how you were designed to function, you are on your way to short-circuiting. You will never release your potential unless you learn to function by faith according to God's specifications.

Key #3—You must know your purpose.

When a manufacturer proposes a new product, he first clarifies the purpose of that product. Then he designs the features to accomplish his intent. Therefore, a car manufacturer will first decide whether the vehicle is to be a race car, a delivery van or a family car. Once the vehicle's purpose has been established, the engineer will incorporate various features to meet that purpose.

Before you were born, God had a plan and a purpose for your life. Then, in accordance with that plan, He gave you special abilities and aptitudes to enable you to accomplish everything that He intended. If you are going to release your potential, you must first discover God's plan for your life. Knowing and living within God's purpose is the difference between using and abusing the gifts and capabilities God built into you.

Key #4—You must understand your resources.

Manufacturers also determine the resources that are necessary for a product to perform correctly and efficiently. A car manufacturer might specify the octane of the gasoline to be used, the pressure of the air in the tires or the weight of the oil for the engine.

God's pattern for your life also includes specifications for the spiritual, physical, material and soul resources that are necessary for you to live a fulfilling and productive life. Until you learn what resources God has arranged for you to enjoy, and what benefits He planned for you to receive from each resource, your potential will be stunted and your performance will be less than it could be.

Key #5—You must have the right environment.

Product engineers consider carefully both the ideal environment under which a product should operate and any unfavorable conditions that might influence the product's performance. While a car manufacturer might establish the ideal conditions as a sunny day with temperatures between 32 and 70 degrees, the engineer must also plan for rainy days, fog, new moon nights and freezing or sweltering temperatures.

When God created human beings, He placed them in the Garden of Eden, where ideal conditions for man's growth and fulfillment were present. When sin entered the world through Adam and Eve's disobedience, man's environment became polluted. But most men and women are not aware of the nature or the proliferation of the pollutants that have invaded their environment. The release of your potential requires both a knowledge of the specifications of the ideal environment God provided in the Garden of Eden and a willingness to make the necessary changes to conform your surroundings to God's specifications.

Key #6—You must work out your potential.

Most products do not achieve their purpose just by virtue of their existence. They have to *do* something to meet the expectations of their manufacturer. A car, for example, must transport its occupants and cargo from point A to point B. Thus, its purpose cannot be fulfilled by sitting in the driveway. The potential to fulfill its purpose is present while it sits in the driveway, but the actual achievement of the manufacturer's intent occurs only when the car *does* what it was designed to do.

God placed Adam in an ideal environment where all the necessary resources for a productive and satisfying life were available to him. Adam enjoyed an intimate relationship with God in which the nature of God, the manner in which God functioned and the purpose for which God had created man were known to Adam. But Adam's potential would have remained locked inside him if God had not given him a job to do. Only through work was Adam's potential to name the animals revealed. The same is true for you. Your potential will not be released until you take your thoughts, plans and imaginations and put them into action. You must work to mine your hidden potential.

Keys to Maximizing Your Potential

Plants are wonderful to watch. After the seeds are buried in the ground, gardeners wait with anticipation for the young shoots to push their way through the soil. Under ideal conditions, most seeds will germinate in a week or two. Although good care is essential during those early weeks of growth, the gardener will not see the full potential of the plants until they begin to bear fruit.

Many times we are initially excited by the glimpses God gives us of the potential He planted within us. In the early weeks and months after we invite Jesus into our hearts, we may spend time in worship, prayer and Bible study; we may attempt to look beyond our present circumstances to the unseen world of faith; we may seek God's guidance in our daily decisions as we open ourselves to His plans and purposes for our lives; we may appreciate and treasure the many blessings He showers upon us; we may carefully adjust our surroundings to make them uplifting and positive; and we may work to bring our dreams and ideas to completion. But as time passes, the garden of our potential loses its early vitality as we allow circumstances and responsibilities to crowd and choke the imaginations and the possibilities that lie hidden within us.

Perhaps you are tapping some of the wealth God stored in you for the world's benefit, but your progress is slowing or even stopping. The following standards are keys to encouraging your garden to maturity as you liberate all the potential that God deposited in you.

Key #1—You must cultivate your potential.

Experienced gardeners know that weeds often grow faster than vegetables. If a gardener goes away for several weeks, he will return to stunted and sickly vegetable plants that yield little or no fruit. Or even worse, he may find that he has no vegetable plants at all because the weeds smothered and choked the tender shoots. Cultivation is necessary for a healthy and productive garden.

The same is true of your potential. You need to cultivate your life carefully to remove the influences and the stimulants that seek to stunt your potential or kill it completely. Seek those persons who are positive and encouraging. Remove yourself from those activities and situations that might encourage you to return to your former way of life. Cling to your Source and allow Him to cleanse you of those things that would deter you from maximizing your potential. *Much emerging potential dies for want of cultivation.* The careful and consistent nurturing of your potential will enable you to meet the full responsibilities that God planned for your life.

Key #2—You must guard your potential.

Most gardeners have experienced the frustration and the disappointment that occur when rabbits, insects or birds destroy their carefully cultivated plants. Fences, insecticides and scarecrows are some of the many things they use to protect young plants from those things that would seek to devour them.

Satan is intent on destroying your potential. He is constantly trying to use a multitude of circumstances, attitudes, things and people to devour your abilities. You will never see but a small portion of what you can do unless you guard your hidden wealth. The release of your full potential is directly dependent on your diligence in protecting your dreams, plans and imaginations from the many negative influences that would block their effective fulfillment.

Key #3—You must share your potential.

Gardening is a shared effort. While the gardener tills the ground, plants the seeds and pulls the weeds, the plants will not bear fruit unless the bees pollinate the blossoms, the sun warms the earth and the rain enables the soil to release its nutrients.

Maximizing your potential and the potential of the billions of people on earth is also a shared effort. *Potential is given for the benefit of many, not for the benefit of one.* There's not much gratification in writing a symphony if no musicians will share their talents to play the music. Nor will the experience of playing the music provide full satisfaction unless an appreciative audience fills the concert hall.

Potential is given for the benefit of many, not for the benefit of one.

God made human beings to live in fellowship with Himself and other human beings. A loveless life that keeps all its accomplishments to itself will soon lose the inspiration for releasing its potential. If you give freely of your gifts, aspirations and abilities, your potential will be magnified and maximized.

Key #4—You must know and understand the laws of limitation.

Every experienced gardener knows that there are numerous laws that affect the success or failure of a garden.

Tender plants wilt in the hot sun when they are planted at noon. Inferior fruit or no fruit results when the plants are not watered regularly. Plants left to the mercy of the weeds yield a lesser crop than those that grow in a weed-free environment. While the gardener is free to ignore those laws, he does not have the power to remove the consequences of his actions.

The same is true for your potential. God has given you the freedom and the power to maximize your potential. He has established laws and commandments to protect your potential, and He has given you the freedom to choose either to obey or disobey them. God has also granted you the power to dream and plan and imagine, along with the responsibility to work those imaginations to fruition. Freedom without law results in purposeless. Power without responsibility is ineffective. Each requires the other to forestall disaster. The outworking of your full potential requires that you understand and abide by the laws and the standards God has set to ensure the full and maximum release of your potential.

PRINCIPLES THAT GOVERN POTENTIAL

1. What God speaks to is the source for what He creates.

2. All things have the same components and essence as the source from which they came.

3. All things must be maintained by the sources from which they came.

4. The potential of all things is related to the sources from which they came.

5. Everything in life has the potential to fulfill its purpose.

6. Potential is determined and revealed by the demands placed on it by its creator.

KEYS TO RELEASING YOUR POTENTIAL

1. You must know your Source.

2. You must understand how you were designed to function.

3. You must know your purpose.

4. You must understand your resources.

5. You must have the right environment.

6. You must work out your potential.

PRINCIPLES

---

1. You came from God.

2. You share the nature and essence of God.

3. You will die unless you remain attached to God.

4. Your potential is determined by God's potential.

5. God gave you the ability to fulfill your potential.

6. You can do what God demands of you because He would not require it if He had not built the power to perform it into you.

5 The Foundation Key

You were created to release God's potential. The source of a resource determines its potential.

Potential is determined and released by the demands made on it by its creator. These demands are based on the design and the components the manufacturer uses to create the product. Thus, when an inventor requires his invention to do something, he demands no more than the ability he built into the invention.

The Impact of Source on Your Potential

God has designed you to release and maximize your potential. But this is possible only when you are related to your Source. Why? Because the source of a product determines the components, essence and nature of the product. Apart from its source, a product cannot know what it's supposed to be or how it was designed to act. God, your Source/Creator, established before your birth who you are, how you should act, why He gave you life, and what you need to live fully and productively. Apart from Him, you will never understand or release your potential, because your potential is wrapped up in Him.

Your Source/Creator determines who you are.

When you became a Christian, God changed your name. He said, "I know you aren't acting like My child, but you are My child. The mess you're in is just a temporary condition. Now that your spirit and My Spirit are reconnected, I can work in you so that your behavior can catch up with your nature. Who you've been is not who you are." The psalmist testifies to this reality.

> [God] **said, "You are 'gods'; you are all sons of the Most High"** (Psalm 82:6).

God doesn't say that we are gods because He is trying to elevate our status. He is stating a fact. The Apostle Peter, in his second letter, amplifies this concept.

> [God's] **divine power has given us everything we need for life and godliness through our knowledge of Him who called us by His own glory and goodness. Through these He has given us His very great and precious promises, so that through them you may participate in the divine nature and escape the corruption in the world caused by evil desires** (2 Peter 1:3-4).

When God created human beings, He intended that we should share *His divine nature*. That is still His intent, even though sin has covered over that nature. Thus, Peter encourages us to live up to our divine nature, because if we operate according to God's nature, we will escape all the temptations and the pressures that come against us in our daily lives. God designed us to be holy and good and forgiving, because they are characteristics of His nature, and we share that nature. When we reconnect with God, we naturally have the power to be all that He is.

Do you know what got Jesus into trouble with the religious authorities? He was too natural! He didn't keep all the rules and the regulations by which the Jewish leaders judged spirituality, yet He had the audacity to say, "God and I are tight." Jesus naturally lived from God's perspective.

You are supposed to be naturally like your Source. God's commands do not require you to live supernaturally, but naturally. If you are a Christian, your natural mode of operation is the same as God's because you came out of Him, and the product always has the nature of its source. That's why God is not impressed when you keep your body free from drugs and your mind free from impure thoughts, or when you give generously, or when you fast and pray. God expects you to act and think like He does because He is your Source/Creator and you are His child.

**God's commands do not require you
to live supernaturally, but naturally.**

Your Source/Creator determines what you can do.

What you can do is related to where you came from. God is serious when He says, "Without Me you can do nothing." It's not a matter of being spiritual, it just plain business sense. He created and made you. You came from Him. Therefore, the quality of your abilities is defined by God's abilities. If you want to know what you can do, find out what God can do.

God, who is omnipotent, created you to share His potential. When He took you out of Himself, He automatically gave you the ability to be creative and imaginative. You share God's potential to plan, design and bring dreams into reality. God is full of more projects, ambitions and proposals than you can imagine. He's the God of the impossible. But He has tied the revelation of His potential to your dreams, aspirations and prayers. That's why God is constantly challenging you to ask Him for the impossible. The possible is no fun for God. He's already done that. It's the ideas, plans and objectives the world hasn't seen yet that God wants to do.

**God has tied the revelation of His potential
to your dreams, aspirations and prayers.**

You are the key to God's creative expression. You can do anything God demands of you because your Creator will never demand more of you than He's already built into you. God's saying to *you*, "Go ahead. Imagine anything you want. There's nothing you can imagine that I don't already have. I need your imagination to demand it. Your potential is related to My potential, and I am omnipotent."

Your Source/Creator determines how you function.

Revelation is God commanding us to demand Him to do what we know no one else can do. It's okay to ask God for something you've already seen Him do; but God wants to do much more than that. God loves faith. That's His mode of operation. It's also yours. God designed you to operate like He does. Faith is going into the realm where you demand out of God what's in Him that no one has seen yet.

**It's okay to ask God for something
you've already seen Him do;
but God wants to do much more than that.**

Are you in a fix no one escaped before? Do you have a problem that no one has ever resolved? Are you in a situation that completely baffles you so that you don't know where to turn? You are the perfect candidate through which God can reveal His glory.

I used to walk around saying, "Well, He did it for her, so He'll do it for me." I don't say that any more. I now know that God will do for me something He's never done before. The richness of God's potential is eternal. Nothing was created without Him.

God gets the glory when you make demands on Him. If you want to glorify God, make Him do things He hasn't done yet. Go out on a limb and stretch your faith. That's how He created you to function. Without faith you cannot please God (Hebrews 11:6). He demands you to perform the way He does, and He operates by faith.

Your Source/Creator determines why you exist.

You will never know your purpose unless you figure out why God created you. Only God knows your purpose, because He determined it when He gave you life. You are not an accident. Psalm 139 describes how God saw your unformed body and ordained your days before you drew your first breath. He planned before you were born what He wanted you to accomplish.

The direction you need to live a satisfying and rewarding life cannot be found in your family, your teachers, your employer, your pastor or your coworkers. They are creatures even as you are. They cannot tell you the reason you were born because they were not present when God put your spirit into your body. They are not privileged to God's thoughts and intentions. *The only way you can discover your purpose is through a relationship with the One who made you.* God's original desires for you shape your potential because He designed you with care to meet the demands He wants to make on you. The release of your total potential requires that you continually seek God as you try to understand what He had in mind when He laid out His plans for your life.

Your Source/Creator determines the resources you need for optimum performance.

Jesus tells the story of a man who was going on a journey. Before he left home, the master called his servants to him and gave each of them a portion of his resources. When he returned, he asked each servant to give an accounting of what they had received. Although the master didn't expect each servant to have equal resources when he returned, he did expect that they would have used and increased the property he had entrusted to them (Matthew 25:14-30).

God has determined the resources you need to live a happy, productive life, because He is the only One who knows what you need to meet the demands He will place upon you. If you are constantly comparing your resources with those of other people, you will be blinded both to the richness of what God has entrusted to you and the tasks He wants you to accomplish using what you have. The release of your full potential demands that you examine your life carefully so you can identify both the many assets God has given you and the purpose for which He gave them. God will not entrust you with more resources until you use wisely what He's already given you.

God will not entrust you with more resources until you use wisely what He's already given you.

Your Source/Creator determines the conditions you need for optimum performance.

Your Creator/Source is the only One who is qualified to define your optimal environment. He does so through His laws and commandments. God's laws establish the elements of your ideal environment and set the necessary requirements for consistent, healthy growth. *God's commandments help you to maintain your environment.* They serve as indicators of the state of your health and the condition of your environment. Your well-being is dependent upon your understanding of God's laws and your obedience to His commandments. You can't afford to break God's commandments because disobedience brings a polluted environment, which stunts and impedes the release of your potential.

You have the potential to perform great exploits for God. But if you fail to maintain the environment God decrees, nothing will happen in your life. It doesn't matter how much you brag about what you can do or what you would like to do, or how much you can see and dream and imagine, if God's requirements aren't met, you aren't going to expose your true self!

Your Source/Creator determines the method(s) by which you fulfill your potential (doing what you were designed to do).

God not only wants to share with you His plans for your life, He also wants you to understand the variety of experiences that He deems necessary for you to effectively fulfill those plans. Many people try one thing after another as they search for the meaning of their lives. They move from one job to the next, from one church to the next, from one town to the next, and from one spouse to the next. When the going gets a little rough, they move on to something else. They never hang in there long enough to make any progress.

Jesus tells a story about a woman who swept her house and searched carefully until she found the coin she had lost (Luke 15:8-10). She didn't just sit in her chair and mourn her loss; she got up and worked until she found it. She translated her desire into a plan, and her plan into *action*. The release of your potential requires that you stick with something until you see it through. It's not enough just to *think* about what God wants from your life, you have to get up and *do* it.

Work is the method God established to release His potential. The creation story tells us that God worked so hard creating the world that He was tired when He finished. Because you came out of God, work is also required of you to bring forth all the invisible jewels that lay hidden inside you.

God established work as a priority that brings fulfillment and contentment. *He designed you to work out your potential.*

A Lesson From Sony

Sony is a Japanese company that manufactures electronics. When you buy an appliance from Sony, you will find a booklet entitled "Operating Instructions" in the top of the box. In the bag with the instruction book you will also find a small slip of paper that says, *"Before disengaging or operating this machine, read these instructions carefully."* Because Sony wants you to experience the maximum enjoyment from its product, the company wants you to be thoroughly familiar with the quality and the capabilities of the machine *before you use it.* If you don't read the manual first, you will never see the high quality and maximum performance that Sony built into the equipment.

The same is true of the highly sophisticated equipment God designed called men and women. You will never reach your optimal performance unless you first check God's operating instructions. The Bible is God's manual on you. You cannot operate properly until you become acquainted with everything God built into you.

One of the first pages in the Sony manual says "Owner's Record" at the top. This page instructs you to *locate the machine's serial number* at the rear of the tape recorder in the battery compartment and *record that number in the space provided below.*

The serial number of a product separates it from all other equipment of that same make and model. The day you invited Jesus into your heart you began a journey that is uniquely yours. Your personality traits and your life experiences have influenced both that moment of decision and your life in Christ since that day. No one else needed Jesus in just the way you did. No one else can experience

His presence and forgiveness in the exact way you did. Record the day you got saved in the front of your Bible. Make some notes about the difference that decision has made in your life. Then continue to check your progress by keeping a diary of your growth. Your history with God is unique. Keep track of your serial number.

The early pages in the book of Sony also include a list of *specifications*. This list details each part of the equipment and tells you what to do if a certain part needs to be replaced. These instructions always include the phrase: *"If service is required, please take or send this product to an authorized dealer who will use genuine Sony parts."*

The Bible details your specifications. God designed you to be filled with the Holy Spirit. If you become filled with a demon spirit or some other foul spirit, you will not function in accordance with God's intentions. That's why a man without God is a dangerous man. He is literally insane. Even though a man's manners may be good, if his spirit is wrong, his behavior will eventually reflect his spirit.

A man without God is a dangerous man.

Never confuse behavior with regeneration. Your behavior is a result of the conversion of your thinking. Regeneration is the source of that conversion. You cannot demand righteousness from an unrighteous spirit. That's why God gives you His Spirit when you come back to Him. Proper behavior is impossible without the Holy Spirit because your functions arise from the nature of your spirit. If you want to function by love, you have to have the Spirit who is the Source of love.

The book of Sony also contains a list of the *features* Sony built into the equipment. The features specified by Sony for a tape recorder might include a voice-operated recording system, an auxiliary microphone jack, a four-source power supply and controls that determine playback speed and review functions.

God has created you with certain features that He has defined and clarified in His operating manual. You have a body, a soul and a spirit. *If you want to operate up to your full potential, you must carefully study how God designed each of these features to function.* There are certain laws that govern each characteristic. If you disregard these laws, you cannot function properly.

Sony also details the *precautions* to be observed when you operate the equipment. These are the don'ts you must avoid if you want to enjoy the highest quality and the maximum performance from the tape recorder. The booklet may *caution* you not to disassemble the casing and to go to a qualified service agent if the equipment is malfunctioning. It also *warns* you that certain things may prevent the machine from recording.

When God created man, He put him in a beautiful garden and gave him authority over all that was in the garden. Then God gave man a *precaution*: "You can eat from all the trees in the garden except for this one tree. If you eat from this tree you will die." *God's precaution was an act of love.* He wanted to save man from the penalties of sin and death. But man violated God's precaution. We are still living with the consequences of that disobedience.

If God gives you a precaution, don't test it to see what will happen if you do it. *Precautions always indicate the consequences of specific actions.* Disobedience is always followed by the assessment of the penalty.

Finally, the operating manual describes the *manufacturer's warranty* and the limitations to that warranty. The manufacturer's warranty guarantees that you can return the product to the manufacturer for repair or replacement if the product fails during the specified warranty period. If, however, you violate the warranty limitations, Sony is no longer responsible for the equipment. You are. These limitations refer primarily to the operation, environment and maintenance of the equipment.

God's warranty includes a clause of grace. He'll take you in your wrecked state and throw out satan's parts. Though it may take years, God will continue to work on your memory banks until your mind is cleaned and your life is transformed. Thank God for His grace. He will pay for all the costs to fix you so long as you go to the right dealer. But you can't expect God to fix you if you are going to satan for repair.

**You can't expect God to fix you
if you are going to satan for repair.**

The last thing Sony tells you in the operating instructions is to *retain the manual for future reference.* In other words, don't throw away your Bibles. You need God's manual to answer the operational questions you will meet in your daily life. You can function three thousand percent better than you are now functioning, so don't get rid of God's manual. The Bible contains the answers for a fulfilling, productive life.

The omnipotent God is your Source/Creator. His instruction manual details the requirements, guidelines and warnings upon which your very life depends. God's life isn't dependent on you. He's alive without you. But your life is dependent on Him. You need Him to find true life. A relationship with God through Jesus Christ, His Son, is the gateway to a full and rich life. He is the foundational key to understanding and releasing your potential. Knowing Him and His intent for your life is the basis for an effective life.

PRINCIPLES

---

1. God wants you to share His divine nature.

2. You are the key to God's creative expression.

3. God designed you to operate by faith.

4. God has a plan for your life.

5. You must have a relationship with your Creator to discover your purpose.

6. You have the potential to do great things for God.

7. Work is the method God established to release your potential.

8. The Bible is God's manual on you. You need to know and heed the requirements, guidelines and warnings it contains.

6 | Know Your Source

Your ability depends on your response to God's ability.

The basic principles that apply to the potential of all things also apply to your potential. God, your Source/Creator, is the Definer of your potential. Because you came from God and share His essence and components, your value and potential are known to Him alone.

Only God Knows Your Value and Potential

Throughout the history of mankind, God has sought to overcome the blindness that sin has brought to our lives. He watches with sadness as His creations discount their potential and doubt their worth. He cries with and for them as they stumble along, missing the many ways He affirms and confirms the valuable persons He created them to be.

The boundaries of what God can accomplish through you were set long before you were born. He planned your days before you had lived even one of them (Psalm 139:16). God wants you to see yourself and your abilities the way He sees you. He puts great value on you and eagerly encourages each step you take toward using even a small part of your talents and abilities. God believes in you. The Bible has much to say about your personal worth and your unique capabilities.

God's Word on Your Value

The Bible is the story of God's interaction with man. It contains many promises from God to His people, as well as the demands God makes on those who would live in fellowship with Him. The Bible also reveals how God sees human beings and their capabilities. God, by sending His Son, shows us the value He places on us. His willingness to send Jesus to die for our sins is the proof of how much we are worth.

When you go to the store to buy a product, you don't put a value on that product. The value of the merchandise was established long before you chose to buy it. When the courtroom of the universe demanded a price for humanity, the value that was placed on the human soul was equal to the death of God. I didn't say the value of the death of God was equal to the human soul. I said that the human soul was equal to the value of the death of God. In other words, God said, "Whatever it costs to restore the fellowship between men and women and Myself, that's the price I will pay." It's not what is paid that gives value to an item, but what it costs.

**It's not what is paid that gives value
to an item, but what it costs.**

Do you understand how much you are worth? You are equal to the value of your Source. You are as valuable as the God you came from! Stop feeling bad about other people's estimations of your value. You are special. You are worth feeling good about. God's word on your potential is the only evaluation that counts. You are not what your teacher or your spouse or your children or your boss say about you. *You are as valuable and capable as God says you are.* If you are going to release your full potential, you must understand and accept the value God places upon you and the confidence He has in your abilities.

God's Word on Your Potential

Even as God is the One who set your value, so too He is the only One who is qualified to determine the extent of your potential. The possibilities that lie within you are dependent upon God, because the potential of a thing is always determined by the source from which it came. Even as the potential of a wooden table is determined by the strength of the tree from which it was made, so your potential is determined by God, because you came out of God. God's Word contains numerous statements that clearly define His evaluation of your potential.

You are in God's class because you are spirit.

Do you remember the process by which God created the world? God first planned what He wanted to create, then He decided what He wanted it to be made from, then He spoke to what He wanted it made out, and what He spoke came forth from what He spoke to. When God wanted animals, for example, He spoke to the dirt because that's what He wanted animals to be made of. Obviously, God did not want you and me to be made of dirt or water or the gases of the air, because He did not speak to the ground or the water or the air. He, who is Spirit, spoke to Himself:

> **Then God said, "Let Us make man in Our** *image..."*
> (Genesis 1:26)

The source to which God spoke when He created man reveals that God wanted us to be like He is.

Now if we further examine the stories of man's creation as recorded in Genesis chapters one and two, we discover that God used two kinds of operations when He called the world into being. He *made* things and He *created* things. The Hebrew word for "make" is *asha*, which means "to form out of something that is already there." *Brera*, the Hebrew word for "create," means "to form out of nothing." It is interesting, then, that Genesis 1:26 says, "Let Us *make* man in Our image..." and the following verse says, "So God *created* man in His own image..." The creation of man thus involved two different operations. God *created* man out of nothing, which is Himself, then He formed man's house from the dust of the ground. After man's house was completed, God took what He had created and put it inside what He had made. Therefore, man came out of God and is spirit even as God is Spirit. The house, which is your body, will decay and return to the ground from which it came. Your spirit, which is your true essence, will live forever because spirits cannot die. You share God's eternal Spirit, with all the dreams, aspirations and desires He contains.

You can operate like God operates.

God also created us to operate like He does:

Then God said, "Let Us make man in Our image, in Our *likeness..."* (Genesis 1:26)

The Hebrew word translated into the English word *like-ness* means "to operate like," not "to look like." God's original design for man requires that we function like God.

Adam and Eve's fall from their initial relationship with God blinded them to their natural mode of operation. Since then, men and women have had difficulty figuring out how they are supposed to act. Instead of cooperating with God, we live in opposition to Him, following the influences of satanic forces.

How does God operate?

God operates by faith. The light in the darkness was not visible before God called it forth, but He believed that light was present in the darkness and, by faith, He spoke it into view. Faith isn't a jump in the dark. It is a walk in the light. Faith is not guessing; it is knowing something.

**Faith isn't a jump in the dark.
It is a walk in the light.
Faith is not guessing; it is knowing something.**

God made and fashioned you to operate by faith. He designed you to believe the invisible into becoming visible. You may not see what God is calling forth from your life, but God asks you to believe it is there. He created you to operate like He does. If you aren't functioning like God, you are malfunctioning. The manual says, "The just shall live by faith" (Romans 1:17), and "everything that does not come from faith is sin [missing the Manufacturer's standards and expectations]" (Romans 14:23).

You can dominate, rule and subdue the earth.

God's perspective on our potential also says that we have the power to dominate and subdue the earth.

> Then God said, "Let Us make man in Our image, in Our likeness, and *let them rule over* the fish of the sea and the birds of the air, over the livestock, over all the earth, and over all the creatures that move along the ground" (Genesis 1:26).

Now what does it mean to be a dominator of the earth? It means that the earth should not rule or control us. If you are addicted to cigarettes, you are being controlled by a leaf. If you are ruled by alcohol, you are being controlled by grain. Leaves and grain are the earth. God created *you* to dominate *the earth*, not the earth to dominate you. If you are being controlled by any habit, you are submitting to the very things God commands you to dominate.

The Apostle Paul confirms God's intent for man when he writes:

> **I beat my body and make it my slave so that after I have preached to others, I myself will not be disqualified for the prize** (1 Corinthians 9:27).

He's telling you to use your head. There are things in the earth that will rule you if you allow them to take control of your physical body. He further states this principle in First Corinthians 6:12:

> **"Everything is permissible for me"—but not everything is beneficial. "Everything is permissible for me"—but I will not be mastered by anything.**

God's given you the potential to dominate the earth. You have the power to beat whatever habit is ruling you. It's there whether you use it or not. Your ability to release the full purpose for which God created you is dependent on your decision to *use* the potential God gave you to control those things that seek to entrap and subdue you. It's up to you whether you exercise the power God built into you.

You can be fruitful and multiply.

God gave every human being the potential to be fruitful and to reproduce after their kind.

> **God blessed them and said to them, *"Be fruitful and increase in number*; fill the earth and subdue it. Rule over the fish of the sea and the birds of the air and over every living creature that moves on the ground** (Genesis 1:28).

While it is true that God gave us the ability to have children, the potential God is talking about here is much more than the capacity to have babies. He has given men and women the potential to reproduce what they are. We are producing the next generation.

What kind of children are you producing? God has given you the power to influence them either for good or for evil. Will the next generation be cussing, alcoholic, illiterate people? Or will they be righteous and upright, seeking the Lord and obeying His commandments? You have the capacity to produce children that mirror your life.

You can plan to do and be anything.

God has also given human beings the capacity to imagine and plan and believe anything into reality. That's an awesome potential. The Bible reveals this power in the story of the building of the tower of Babel:

> **The Lord said, "If as one people speaking the same language they have begun to do this, then nothing they plan to do will be impossible for them"** (Genesis 11:6).

In other words, God says, "If I don't interfere, man will be able to do anything he thinks about and plans."

God did interfere in the building of that tower, but He didn't stop the people from thinking. He stopped them from understanding one another. You have the potential to think, to imagine, to plan and to put your plan into action. Anything you carry through from thought to action is within your power to accomplish.

You can accomplish impossibilities.

Consistent with man's ability to make plans and bring them to completion is his power to believe impossibilities into possibilities. Jesus said to the father of a demon-possessed boy:

Everything is possible for him who believes (Mark 9:23).

This ability is an extension of man's potential to operate like God.

The Gospel of Matthew tells a story of faith in which one of Jesus' disciples, for a moment, accomplished the impossible. Peter, with the other disciples, was in a boat on the Sea of Galilee when Jesus came to them, walking on the water. The disciples, thinking it was a ghost, cried out in fear. After Jesus had identified Himself, impetuous Peter replied, "Lord, if it's You...tell me to come to You on the water" (Matthew 14:28).

Now you and I know that the physical laws of nature should have prevented Peter from walking to Jesus. But the laws of faith are different. When Jesus told him to come, Peter got out of the boat and went toward Jesus. Only when he became fearful of the wind and the waves did he begin to sink. "Immediately Jesus reached out His hand and caught him. 'You of little faith,' He said, 'why did you doubt?' " (Matthew 14:31)

If you are a man or woman of faith, you have the awesome power to operate by the laws of faith. Impossibilities become possibilities when you use this potential.

You can influence things on earth and in heaven.

Man's tremendous potential also includes the capacity to influence both physical and spiritual things. This capacity is a colossal power that we seldom use. Jesus pointed to this power when He told Peter (after Peter had confessed, "You are the Christ, the Son of the living God" [Matthew 16:16]):

Blessed are you, Simon son of Jonah, for this was not revealed to you by man, but by My Father in heaven. And I tell you that you are Peter, and on this rock I will build My church, and the gates of Hades will not overcome it.

I will give you the keys of the kingdom of heaven; whatever you bind on earth will be bound in heaven, and whatever you loose on earth will be loosed in heaven (Matthew 16:17-19).

Jesus is encouraging us to look beyond the physical circumstances of our lives to the spiritual dimension. If you are dealing with just the physical aspects of your life, you are missing the real thing. Look beyond the problems in your job or with your spouse or in your church to the spiritual realities that underlie them. Say in the natural what you want to happen in the spiritual. The power to affect both realms is yours. You hold the keys to your effective participation in God's Kingdom, because all authority in heaven and on earth belongs to Jesus (Matthew 28:18), and He has shared that power with you.

**If you are dealing with just
the physical aspects of your life,
you are missing the real thing.**

You can receive whatever you ask.

During His time on earth, Jesus gave His disciples a blank check. He promised them that they could receive whatever they requested.

Therefore I tell you, whatever you ask for in prayer, believe that you have received it, and it will be yours (Mark 11:24).

If you remain in Me and My words remain in you, ask whatever you wish, and it will be given you. This is to My Father's glory, that you bear much fruit, showing yourselves to be My disciples (John 15:7-8).

Jesus cautioned His disciples that the evidence of fruit in their lives would be the indicator that they were His disciples. He also established the key to bearing fruit as their willingness to remain in touch with Him. In so far as you remain in touch with your Creator/Source, you have the power to ask whatever you wish and to receive what you request. That's God's promise concerning your potential. He's waiting to give you whatever you request, so long as you sink your roots deep into His Word and allow His words to influence and direct your entire life.

You have the power to do greater works than Jesus did.

During His last days on earth, Jesus spent much time with His disciples teaching them, praying for them and encouraging them to live in His power. As He spoke of His return to the Father, Jesus assured His disciples that they would continue the work He had begun because they would receive the same power they had witnessed in His ministry (Acts 1:8).

> **Believe Me when I say that I am in the Father and the Father is in Me; or at least believe on the evidence of the miracles themselves. I tell you the truth, anyone who has faith in Me will do what I have been doing. He will do even greater things than these, because I am going to the Father. And I will do whatever you ask in My name, so that the Son may bring glory to the Father. You may ask Me for anything in My name, and I will do it** (John 14:11-14).

We usually measure those works in terms of the height of the water we will walk on or the number of people we will feed from a few groceries. That is, we interpret Jesus' words to mean that we will do *more* works, when that was not His intent.

Jesus was one man in one body with the Spirit of God living inside Him. His ministry consisted of that which He could accomplish as one person, in a specific geographic area, at a certain point in history. After Jesus' death and His return to the Father, the Spirit of God was freed to fill millions of people, not just one. The book of Acts tells the story of the Spirit's outpouring on the early Church.

When Jesus foretold that His disciples would do greater works than He had done, He was talking about the baptism of the Holy Spirit and the power that outpouring would bring into their lives. If you have received Jesus as your Savior, and the Holy Spirit is operative in your life, you have the potential to share in the Church's commission to do greater works than Jesus did. *Therefore, the greater works did not refer to greater in quality, but in quantity and dimension.* These works were no longer limited to one body or one geographical location, but became worldwide. What potential!

Your Potential Is Dependent Upon God

Some people believe that God is afraid we're going to take His job. When we start talking about what we're going to do for God or what we're going to dream, some people say, "You'd better not think bigger than God." Well, you can never be bigger than your Source. *You can't think or plan or imagine something greater than God, because God is the source of your imagination.* He leaked part of His potential into you when He pulled you out of Himself. It's like owning a Sony video cassette recorder with multiple features. It cannot fulfill its purpose or potential until it is plugged into an electrical source. So it is for every man. We must plug into our Source

It is imperative, then, that you understand the characteristics and qualities of God, as well as the provisions He has made to enable you to fulfill the purpose for which He created you. *Your ability to release your potential is directly related to your knowledge of God and your willingness to stay within the parameters He has established for your relationship with Him.*

You must know the qualities and the nature of God.

Quality is the degree of excellence or the essence of standard that makes one product better than another. The quality of a product can be no better than the qualities of the product's source. You can't use rotten apples to make a delicious apple pie. The pie will reveal the decay in the apples.

The quality of a product can also be defined as the characteristic attributes or elements that determine the product's basic nature. Those qualities arise out of the basic nature of the product's source. Or to say it another way, those things that occur naturally in a product also occur naturally in that from which the product was made.

The standards of God are the standards by which your excellence is judged, because you came out of God. Likewise, the characteristics that describe God's basic nature also describe your basic nature. If you want to know what the standards for your life are, check God's standards. If you want to know what characteristics occur in you naturally, ascertain God's inherent qualities. If God acts by a certain standard or exhibits a certain quality, that standard or quality is part of your life as well.

For example, God has the quality of faithfulness. Therefore, you have the ability to be faithful. Because God is unconditional love, you have the characteristic of love somewhere under all your hatred. Because God is merciful and long-suffering, you can be merciful and long-suffering. All the essential qualities that determine who God is and how He acts also determine who you are and how you were designed to act. Your potential is wrapped up in God because His qualities establish yours. Only when you understand and accept the nature and qualities of God can you begin to understand and accept your nature and qualities.

One of the greatest indicators of your quality and standards is expressed in God's commandments. Whatever He demands of you He knows is inside you. That's why the manual says that His "commandments are not grievous" (1 John 5:3).

You must know God's laws and obey His commandments.

In the second chapter of Genesis, God set a law about Adam's relationship with the trees of the garden: "...if you eat from [the tree of the knowledge of good and evil] you will surely die" (Genesis 2:17). Because of this law, God also gave Adam a command: "You are free to eat from any tree in the garden; but you must not eat from the tree of the knowledge of good and evil..." (Genesis 2:16-17) When Adam disobeyed God, he brought upon himself the reality of the law God had set. He died.

Now the book of Genesis makes it clear that Adam didn't die physically at the moment of his disobedience. He lived to be 930 years old. Adam's disobedience caused his *spiritual* death.

The death of an old tree is a good word picture to describe the nature of Adam's death. When a large tree is blown down by a hurricane, the tree may lay there for weeks. Although the roots of the tree are torn from the ground and exposed to the air, the tree's leaves do not turn brown as soon as the tree is brought down by the wind. The little sap that was in the roots continues to move up the trunk, out the branches and into the leaves. When the sap is gone, the leaves turn brown. But the reality of that tree's death occurred when it fell, not when the leaves showed the evidence of its death.

Adam walked around with green leaves but no roots for many years. He was dead long before his body showed the evidence of his death. All people share Adam's death. Unless your life becomes *rerooted in God* through the salvation offered in Jesus Christ, you are going to die an eternal death. That's the law of God.

The laws of God are many and they carry with them natural results. His commandments are given for our good because they caution us not to disregard God's laws. When Adam broke God's commandment, he experienced the natural results of God's law.

Obedience to God's commandments brings His blessings. The twenty-eighth chapter of Deuteronomy—in the words of Moses to the children of Israel—promises God's blessings for those who obey His commandments:

> **If you fully obey the Lord your God and carefully follow all His commands I give you today, the Lord your God will set you high above all the nations on earth. All these blessings will come upon you and accompany you if you obey the Lord your God** (Deuteronomy 28:1-2).

Your potential is limitless so long as you comprehend God's laws and purpose in your heart to obey His commandments.

You must understand God's potential.

Daniel 11:32 promises that "the people [who] know their God shall be strong, and do exploits" (KJV). This is true because your potential is related to God's potential, and God is *omnipotent*. The combination of *omni* (meaning "always or all full of") and *potent* (meaning "power on reserve"—from which we get the word *potential*) declares that God is always full of power. Or to say it another way, all potential is in God. Thus, people who understand that God contains all the things that He's asking them to do are not afraid to do big things. It's not *what* you know but *who* you know that enables you to do great things with God.

God is God whether you choose to use His potential or not. Your decision to live with Him or without Him does not affect who He is or what He can do. He is not diminished when you choose to replace Him with other sources. God still has the stuff you need to fulfill your potential.

God is God whether you choose
to use His potential or not.

When you combine the knowledge of God's omnipotence with the knowledge of who you are in God, you can resist all things that seek to overcome you and to wipe out your potential. You can be strong and do great exploits. God is the Source of your potential. He waits to draw from His vast store to enable you to accomplish all that He demands of you.

You must have faith in God.

If I give you a tree as a gift and I tell you it is an avocado tree, you will tell every person who asks you what kind of tree is in your front yard that it's an avocado tree. Now you haven't picked any avocados from that tree, but you still dare to say it's an avocado tree. Why? Because you have faith in me that the tree is what I say it is. You believe that somewhere in that tree there are many avocados. Faith is simply believing and acting on the words and integrity of another. Faith in God is to believe and act on what He says.

The words of Jesus as recorded in the Gospel of Mark admonish us to have faith in God.

> **"Have faith in God," Jesus answered. "I tell you the truth, if anyone says to this mountain, 'Go, throw yourself into the sea,' and does not doubt in his heart but believes that what he says will happen, it will be done for him"** (Mark 11:22-23).

What Jesus is really saying is, "Have the God kind of faith." Don't put your faith in your own faith or in the faith of other people or in the mountains or in anything that you expect to happen because of your faith. Put your faith in God, because it's your faith in Him that will accomplish the moving of mountains. You can't speak to the mountain and expect it to move unless you are connected to God. Apart from Him you don't have the power to complete such monumental tasks.

You must stay attached to God.

The book of Colossians describes Jesus as "the image of the invisible God, the firstborn over all creation. For by Him all things were created: things in heaven and on earth, visible and invisible..." (Colossians 1:15-16) Hebrews 1:3 tells us that "the Son is the radiance of God's glory and the exact representation of His being, sustaining all things by His powerful word." The King James Version of this verse says that Jesus upholds all things "by the word of His power..." Not the *power of His word*, but *the word of His power*. God's power is released in you when you stay alive with His word.

When God created plants, He called them forth from the soil, thereby establishing the law that plants must live off the soil. If a plant violates that word, it dies. Thus, God keeps that plant alive by the power of His word. So long as the plant abides by the law God set at creation, it flourishes and grows. If, however, the plant chooses to disregard that law, death is inevitable.

The same is true in our lives. By taking us out of Himself, God decreed that our lives must be maintained by Him. So long as we obey God's requirement, His power is released within us and we know abundant life. That is why the writer to the Hebrews describes Jesus as the "Word of God's power." There's power in God's word if we keep it. Jesus, through His obedience unto death, released for us the power of God's word that brings eternal life.

Jesus looks at this same power from a different perspective when, in the fifteenth chapter of John, He describes Himself as the vine and His disciples as the branches. He used the word picture of the vine because it is the only plant that doesn't have life in its branches. If you clip a branch from a rose bush or a lemon tree, plant it in the soil and give it the proper care, the branch will root and start a new plant. This is not true for the grape vine. There is no life in the branch of a vine. No matter how rich and green it looks, a branch apart from the vine will wither and die.

> **No branch can bear fruit by itself; it must remain in the vine. Neither can you bear fruit unless you remain in Me** (John 15:4).

If you cut yourself off from God, your potential is aborted. No matter how hard you try to plant yourself in other organizations and activities, God says, "You are dead." Even if you plant yourself in *religion*, you are dead unless you know God and draw your nutrients from Him.

Our need for God is not an alternative or an option. Like the plants and the animals, which cannot be maintained without the soil, and the fish, which cannot live outside the water, *we cannot flourish and bear fruit apart from God.* When Jesus says in John 14:6, "I am the way, the truth and the life...," He isn't trying to convince us that He's the *best* way. He didn't use that word. Life rooted in God is a necessity. There is no option. Although you can say to a plant, "You can either stay in the soil or get out of the pot and sit on the windowsill," the plant doesn't really have a choice. If the plant chooses the windowsill, it will die. There is no alternative to the soil for the plant to meet its basic needs. So it is with human beings and God.

If you stay within God's word, His word takes root in your heart and becomes established. His power is released as you stay alive with His word. *If, however, you pull yourself out of God, you shut down your productivity* and forfeit the blessings God wants to give you. You become as limited as the books, people, education, etc. that are feeding your thought patterns.

Do you want joy? Go to God. Do you need peace? Set your roots firmly in the Word and power of God. Do you need help to control your temper? Spend time with God. Jesus promises: "...with God all things are possible" (Matthew 19:26). God is the soil you unconditionally need.

You must cooperate with the Holy Spirit.

God's potential is far greater than anything we can ask Him to do. Everything that is visible came out of God. Everything that we yet will see is still within Him. Because we came out of God, that same potential is available to us. But there's a catch. God's power must be at work within us before we can tap that power.

> Now unto Him who is able to do immeasurably more than all we ask or imagine, according to His power that is at work within us, to Him be glory in the Church and in Christ Jesus throughout all generations, for ever and ever! Amen (Ephesians 3:20-21).

When Jesus told His disciples that He was going away, He promised them that the Holy Spirit would come to be with them forever (John 14:16). Moments before His ascension to Heaven, Jesus also promised that the *power of the Holy Spirit* (Acts 1:8) would equip His followers to be His messengers.

Is the Holy Spirit present in your life? Are you flowing in a consistent, empowering relationship that undergirds your every thought, dream and plan? Or are you trying to do great things without the power of the Spirit?

We may see a skyscraper or a space shuttle or a fancy computer and say, "That's something else. Man is really working here." But the Spirit says, "That's nothing compared to what man could do. That's what man is doing without Me. I want you to do something people cannot do unless they have Me. I want you to build people. I have the stuff to empower you to help people build new foundations and open new windows through which to see life. I want to give you a view from the top of life so you can see the way God sees." Wow! What power! That's the power that must be working inside you if you are going to do great things for God.

Your cooperation with the work of the Holy Spirit is the means by which God reveals the stuff He took from Himself and gave to you. When you are in tune with the Holy Spirit, you can do things this world has never seen. The power's there. It's up to you whether you make the connection that releases the power. If that power isn't working in you, your potential is being wasted.

You must use Christ's strength.

In Philippians 4:13 Paul says,

I can do everything through Him who gives me strength.

You cannot do *all things*. You can only do *all things* through *Christ*, who gives you the ability. Even though you may shout to everybody, "I can do all things," God is asking you, "Are you with Christ?" Because if you're not, your plans, dreams and imaginations will amount to nothing. Without Christ your efforts are futile and the result is frustration.

Romans 8:31 gives me great encouragement: "If God is for us, who can be against us?" Now the word *for* is really the Greek word *with*. So let's put it this way: "If God is with me, who can be against me?" The implication is that if God has given you something to do and He is with you, nothing or no one is going to stop you from accomplishing what God wants you to do. I don't care who the person is or how much influence he has, if God is with you, it's not important who is coming against you.

If you are going to release your potential, you must live each day checking out who's *with* you instead of who's *against* you. You may be experiencing political victimization, pressure from your boss or your spouse or your parents, or unfair treatment from your family or your employer, but these influences are not the most important factors in your life. You can spend the rest of your life fighting the many people and circumstances that come against you, or you can focus on God's presence and treat them as a temporary inconvenience. If God is with you, those who accuse or harass you have no power over you.

This week can be a good one because your protection relies not on how much power your accusers have but on how much power Christ has. Jesus promises you peace and victory if you rely on His strength:

> **In this world you will have trouble. But take heart! I have overcome the world** (John 16:33).

God is your Source. Without a relationship with God through His Son Jesus, you will forfeit your potential. If you haven't received Jesus as your Lord and Savior, I invite you to pray the following prayer with me in faith:

Dear Heavenly Father,

I understand and accept the truth that You are my Source and the Manufacturer of my life. I acknowledge that I need You just as the plant needs the soil from which it came. I, therefore, submit myself to Your authorized dealers, the Lord Jesus Christ and the Holy Spirit, and receive forgiveness of all my sins. I accept Your promise of the Holy Spirit right now and rejoice that I can be reconciled and restored to the Manufacturer of my life with the full guarantee of eternal life and the unlimited release of my potential. Thank you, Father.

In the name of Jesus, My Lord,
Amen.

PRINCIPLES

---

1. God believes in you and your abilities.

2. You are as valuable and capable as God says you are.

3. You have God's nature and qualities.

4. You can accomplish anything that you carry through from thought to action.

5. You can't think, plan or imagine something greater than God, because God is the Source of your imagination.

6. If you pull yourself out of God, you are dead. He is the soil you unconditionally need.

7 | Understand Your Function

Vision is the ability to see above and beyond the majority.

Man has become an expert at understanding how plants and animals function. We crossbreed animals to create strains that are stronger, tastier and more productive, and we graft stock from one tree to another to develop more compact trees that yield tastier fruit that grow larger and keep longer. But we are deficient in our understanding and application of how God designed man to function. We concentrate on our bodies instead of our spirits. This situation seriously threatens our ability to release our potential.

Designed for Eternity

When God created human beings, He spoke to Himself so that men and women could be spiritual beings even as He is Spirit. He designed them to share His knowledge and wisdom and to understand His thoughts and purposes. God also assigned them part of His potential in that He gave them eternal spirits with eternal plans, ideas and projects.

Death and dirt have become such expected parts of our lives that we don't understand or appreciate the concept of free, abundant, eternal life. We assume that death is natural, and we live as though sin is natural, when in truth God designed us to be holy beings who live forever.

The Result of Disobedience

Adam's disobedience destroyed God's plan and brought alienation between God and man. Because man was no longer sustained by his Source, man's spirit died and his body lost its ability to continually rebuild and replenish itself. Thus, the sin that brought spiritual death also caused physical death: "For the wages of sin is death..." (Romans 6:23)

Man in his fallen state could no longer know and understand the thoughts and purposes of God. He became controlled by his soul instead of his spirit and began to look to his environment for the information he needed. Thus, man without God is a paralyzed spirit in dirt, walking on two legs.

Man without God is a paralyzed spirit in dirt, walking on two legs.

All human beings since Adam sin: "For all have sinned and fall short of the glory of God..." (Romans 3:23) They bear in their spirits, souls and bodies the penalty of his disobedience. You were born spiritually dead or paralyzed, and your body will eventually die. Your brain, apart from God, can know no more than those who teach you or those who write the books you read.

"Mere Dirt"

Your body does not need God to live. It came from the ground and needs the products from the ground to stay alive. Jesus spoke of this when He asked the Pharisees:

"Are you still so dull?" Jesus asked them. "Don't you see that whatever enters the mouth goes into the stomach and then out of the body? But the things that come out of the mouth come from the heart, and these make a man 'unclean.' For out of the heart come evil thoughts, murder, adultery, sexual immorality, theft, false testimony, slander. These are what make a man 'unclean' " (Matthew 15:16-20a).

Psyche, the Greek word translated *heart,* literally means "the core of the spirit." It's what goes into your spirit that destroys you. Cancer may destroy your body, but it can't harm your spirit. True, your spirit may become depressed by the cancer's affects upon your body, but ultimately your spirit will live if you stay attached to God. That's why rebellion against God is such a serious matter. When you detach yourself from your Source, your spirit man dies or enters a state of eternal paralysis, void of relationship and communion with God the Holy Spirit. Then the only thing you have is a decaying body. Life from the body leads to death.

The desire to steal or covet is prompted by what you see with your physical eyes, and your sexual desires are provoked by the physical wants of your body. Indeed, life from the body discourages respect and encourages behavior that regards men and women as objects to be conquered. We are tempted to treat people like products to be manipulated instead of images of Christ to be cherished and honored.

God has a name for those who detach themselves from Him and live from the body. He calls them "mere dirt." Now that's an insult. Any person who doesn't know God is a mere man. A mere person does things unnaturally. Because they don't know their Creator and the purposes and desires He had when He created them, they focus on their *made* beings—that which came from the dust—instead of their *created* beings—that which came from God. They abuse themselves and others because they don't know how God designed them to act. Death and dirt characterize their lives.

God's Plan of Redemption

The God who designed you for eternal life still desires the fellowship with you that He originally intended. He sent Jesus into the world to take away the root problem of your sin so eternity can once more be yours.

> **Therefore, there is now no condemnation for those who are in Christ Jesus, because through Christ Jesus the law of the Spirit of life set me free from the law of sin and death** (Romans 8:1-2).

> **For the wages of sin is death, but the gift of God is eternal life in Christ Jesus our Lord** (Romans 6:23).

God didn't need to save you from sin and death to meet *His* needs. He was doing fine before you were saved, and He'll continue to do fine no matter what kind of relationship you have with Him in the future. Jesus was touched by *your* needs. Only when you recognize that coming to God is for your benefit, not God's, does God's grace make sense. Grace is God reaching out when He didn't need to. Grace is God caring enough to rework His original plan for the fallen race of man:

> **Whoever believes in the Son has eternal life, but whoever rejects the Son will not see life, for God's wrath remains on him** (John 3:36).

The Redemption of Your Spirit

Jesus came to lift you from a life centered around the interests, power and desires of your body to a life centered in God. He came to redeem you and to release your potential by reconnecting your spirit and God's Spirit.

The word *redeemed* means "to purchase again." If you lost a doll and someone found it, she could require you to pay her to get it back. The twenty dollars she asked you to pay would be the "redemptive price" because you would be buying back something that was originally yours.

You were originally God's property, but satan stole you from God. Jesus paid the redemptive price of death on the cross so you could be restored to eternal life and fellowship with God. When Jesus saved you from sin and death, he rekindled your potential spirit by giving you His Holy Spirit to live in you and to be connected to your spirit. Because of that gift, you can begin to flow again in the many things He gave you before you were born. Through Jesus, God renewed your spiritual life and reconnected your soul to His fountain of wisdom and knowledge.

The Redemption of Your Body

Although Jesus redeemed your spirit man, your body has not yet been redeemed. After Jesus rose from the dead, He promised that He would return to redeem your body.

> **Christ has indeed been raised from the dead, the firstfruits of those who have fallen asleep. For since death came through a man, the resurrection of the dead comes also through a man. ... We will not all sleep, but we will all be changed—in a flash, in the twinkling of an eye, at the last trumpet. For the trumpet will sound, the dead will be raised imperishable, and we will be changed** (1 Corinthians 15:20-21,51b-52).

God intended for your body to live forever. The ability of your finger to heal after you burn it, or of an incision to heal following surgery, attests to the small amount of eternal potential left in your body. God still intends that you will have an eternal body. He has promised that He will give life to your body at the resurrection of the dead. Your resurrected body will be like Adam's body before he sinned and

Jesus' body after He rose from the dead. You will be able to touch your new physical body: "Look at My hands and My feet. It is I Myself! Touch Me and see; a ghost does not have flesh and bones, as you see I have" (Luke 24:39), and you will be able to eat: "They gave Him a piece of boiled fish, and He took it and ate it in their presence" (Luke 24:42-43).

In this life, your body is a hindrance. It gets tired, sick, bruised and discouraged. As it grows older, you have to keep patching it together. That's why our society is so eager to find a fountain of youth. We don't like our aging bodies. We want them to be young again.

I like what Paul says in his second letter to the Corinthians:

Therefore we do not lose heart. Though outwardly we are wasting away, yet inwardly we are being renewed day by day (2 Corinthians 4:16).

God's making you a new home that will far exceed anything that plastic surgery can do for you. All plastic surgeons can do is patch your old body. God's in the business of giving you a new body. So don't worry if this body isn't all you'd like it to be. Patch it, fix it, do whatever you can to spruce it up. *But don't equate your life with your body.* God's going to get out of you all that He put in you. He wants you to start releasing your potential with the body you now have and to continue using your eternal capabilities long after this body has decayed. *You are much more than your imperfect, deteriorating body.*

God's System—Faith

God designed you to be a limitless person. He pulled you from His omnipotent Self and transferred to you a portion of His potential. He also wired you to operate like He does. When you reconnect with God through faith in Jesus Christ, He empowers you to return to your original mode of operation, which is like His own.

God thinks in terms of potential—of things that are not yet manifested. He relies on what He knows isn't visible yet, instead of what is visible. He is not excited by what you've already done.

If you've accomplished something, enjoy it and appreciate it. But don't get so hung up on it that you fail to move on to what you yet can do. The Apostle Paul expresses it this way:

> **Forgetting what is behind and straining toward what is ahead, I press on toward the goal to win the prize for which God has called me heavenward in Christ Jesus** (Philippians 3:13-14).

Paul wasn't satisfied with what he had attained. He was always looking for the next step. Why? Because the past is no longer motivational. Only when you look to the future with its demands and challenges can you release more of your untapped talents and abilities.

If God says you *are* or *have* something, it's in you somewhere. He sees what people can't see, and He says what He sees. If God says that you are an overcomer, you are an overcomer. The fact that you look more like an undercomer than an overcomer doesn't change the truth that you are an overcomer. Because God says it, it is true.

God's waiting for your potential to be revealed. He says, "You are not what you are acting like. Because you are My child, you have the potential to act better than you're acting. My potential is flowing from Me to you."

Life From the Spirit or Life From the Body?

Many of us don't appreciate how faith works. We are so used to living from what we can see, hear and touch that we have great difficulty moving into the realm of faith. If, for example, someone asks us how we are doing, we usually respond based on the condition of our bodies or our souls.

We focus on our illnesses or the depressed thoughts that are weighing us down and neglect to mention the many blessings God has promised us. These promises have a much greater impact on our lives than our physical diseases and our emotional struggles.

If someone asks you how you are doing, tell them that you're blessed. You might not look like it, but God's blessings are in you somewhere. And each time that you say you are blessed, the blessings within you grow. Eventually what you say and what you see will match.

Faith sees what hasn't been manifested. It deals with what exists but is invisible. The minute you manifest something, it no longer requires faith, because faith is believing, conceiving and releasing (speaking) until you receive what you desire. "Faith is being sure of what [you] hope for and certain of what [you] do not see" (Hebrews 11:1).

The Faith Process

Faith begins with *belief.* Actually, faith in someone or something requires unquestioning belief that does not require proof or evidence from the one in whom you have faith. The New Testament word for faith, *pistos*, means "to believe another's testimony." Thus, faith requires you to function by believing first, instead of seeing or feeling first.

Faith requires you to function by believing first, instead of seeing or feeling first.

That often creates a problem, because faith requires putting your body under the control of your spirit. Your body says, "I'm not going to believe it until I see it." But God says, "If you're going to operate like Me, you aren't going to see it until you believe it!" Likewise, the world says, "I'll buy shares in your company when I see strong growth," when

God says, "Let's get on *now* with building your business." One operates by sight, the other by faith.

Living by faith also requires that you put your soul under the control of your spirit. Your soul governs your emotions, your will and your mind. When you live from your soul, you allow information from your physical body to govern your decisions. Your soul says, "I'm unhappy because the outward circumstances of my life aren't what I'd like." Just because you don't *feel* what God is saying to you, don't refuse to believe that He knows what He is talking about.

After you believe God's promises, you must begin to *see* (conceive) them in your life. Seeing and looking are very different. Looking regards the outward appearance, while seeing considers the existence of things that are not yet visible. *Many look, but few see.* God sees, and He requires that you see. He asks you to act as though you already have what you requested.

After you can see something, you have to *release* it. In Genesis, God looked at the darkness and saw light. Although the light existed, it was not made visible until God spoke it into being. The same thing happened in the life of a young girl who was visited by the angel Gabriel. Although she was engaged to be married, she had not yet known a man. Imagine her surprise when Gabriel told her that she would give birth to a son who was to be named Jesus. Mary could have argued that this was impossible, but she calmly asked: "How will this be...since I am a virgin?" (Luke 1:34) By faith Mary believed the words of the angel—"The Holy Spirit will come upon you, and the power of the Most High will overshadow you"—and released the birth of Jesus—"May it be to me as you have said."

God is still sending angels to speak things that run contrary to our usual expectations. He says to men and women, "You will have a dream and it will come to pass." Then He waits for our words of confirmation: "May it be to me as

You have spoken." But what you speak must follow what you believe. Words themselves have no power. Only when words are accompanied by belief can they release God's desires for your life. The Apostle Paul illustrated this when he spoke what was already in his heart:

> It is written: "I believed; therefore I have spoken." With that same spirit of faith we also believe and therefore speak, because we know that the one who raised the Lord Jesus from the dead will also raise us with Jesus and present us with you in His presence (2 Corinthians 4:13-14).

Faith is required of all who want to please God. Hebrews 11:6 warns us that "without faith it is impossible to please God, because anyone who comes to Him must believe that He exists and that He rewards those who earnestly seek Him," and Romans 1:17 says, "The righteous will live by faith." You were created to live by faith. God established faith as the only system through which men and women can touch His power. Potential demands faith, and faith makes demands on potential.

**Potential demands faith,
and faith makes demands on potential.**

Righteousness, which, in the Bible, means "to enjoy a right relationship with God," is impossible without God's act of salvation in Jesus Christ. Jesus' death on the cross freed you from eternal death, which is the penalty for your sin. For those who have received new life in Christ, God renders a verdict of "not guilty."

Faith Is a Requirement, Not an Option

Faith is not an option for the Christian. It is a necessity. If God tells you to get moving, He doesn't want you to stand around until you see the evidence that says you should get moving. He wants you to risk, simply because He is asking you to move.

In fact, faith is not an option for human beings in general. A person who lives on anything but faith is going to live a depressing life. He will be so consumed by his environment and the circumstances of his life that he will never venture beyond the known to release the vast potential inside him. Faith is the source of hope, and no man can live without hope. Faith is the fuel of the future and the energy of anticipation.

Faith Makes Things Happen

Many people are wrecks because they try to live without faith. That's unfortunate because the Scriptures are clear that faith in God is the prerequisite for receiving what you believe, conceive and release.

> **Therefore I tell you, whatever you ask for in prayer, believe that you have received it, and it will be yours** (Mark 11:24).

Faith is the catalyst that makes things happen. It lifts you above the outward evidence of your life and empowers you to bring light out of darkness. Remember, you will receive whatever you believe. If you expect trouble, you will get it. If you trust God and expect Him to work in the midst of your distressing circumstances, sooner or later you will see evidence of His presence.

Life without faith is foolish because life is not always what it seems. What you see or feel is not the whole story. Believe that things are going to work out. Reject the garbage that discourages you by taking your eyes off God—"You're never going to own a house. You can't even pay this rent. How're you going to afford a mortgage?"—and believe that you are going to make it. Make plans and, by faith, release your dreams by saying: "I know what I see, but I also know what I believe. I'm going to keep believing in my dreams, because all things are possible with God." Praise Him that you don't have to live by what you see. Believe in His promises and expect Him to move mountains for you (Matthew 21:21).

**Life is not always what it seems.
What you see or feel is not the whole story.**

If things aren't working out for you, there's probably something wrong with your believing, conceiving or speaking. Stop being intimidated by evil influences or the wicked one. Because he doesn't want you to live by faith, the evil one tries to convince you to believe wrong, conceive wrong and speak wrong so there's no way you can receive what you have believed. Refuse to believe his lies and be careful not to worry about the criticisms and objections of others. *If God is the source of your dream, people cannot destroy it.* You can accomplish what God wills.

So get back to God's Word and claim His promises. Make faith the daily foundation of your life and say, "God said, therefore I believe" until you start to see some differences. Above all, don't give up.

Before long you'll see the results of a life of faith. You'll get up in the morning expecting it to be a good day because there's nothing you and God can't handle together. You'll start the week believing God's word and acting on His instructions. That's living by faith. Nothing in this world can make you lose heart unless you allow it to.

The Tragedy of Relinquishing Faith

Most people who are failures, are failures because they were so close to winning. Don't let that happen to you. You don't know how close you are to receiving the promise you have been waiting for. Just because things are getting worse doesn't mean that God has not heard your request. The closer you get to victory, the harder you are going to have to fight. Often when things are the worst, you are close to receiving what you seek.

Set your pace and keep on trucking. Look for the positive in life and renew your voice of faith. Believe in God and in yourself. Say, "God, I'm on Your side, and You're on mine. We are going to see this thing through because we are a majority." Trust in the certainty that you can't lose when you and God are in agreement, and bear in mind that God will reward you if you put Him above all else. Finally, commit yourself to believing, conceiving and releasing (speaking) every day until you receive what you desire. That's how God created you to function.

But seek first His kingdom and His righteousness, and all these things will be given to you as well (Matthew 6:33).

A life of faith is hard work that at times requires perseverance and patience, but you can't live any other way. Faith is the basis upon which an abundant, satisfying life is built. It is an essential key to releasing all that God put in you to benefit yourself and the world for generations to come. Your potential needs faith to draw it out, because faith is the bucket that draws from the well of potential within you.

Faith is the bucket that draws from the well of potential within you.

PRINCIPLES

1. God gave you an eternal spirit with eternal potential.

2. Sin has robbed you of that potential because you are born spiritually dead.

3. God redeemed your eternal potential through the death of Jesus.

4. You were designed to live by faith.

5. Faith is believing, seeing, releasing and receiving.

8 | Understand Your Purpose

Life without purpose is an experiment.

Saul was a zealous Jew who intensely persecuted the early Church and tried to destroy it. But God had another plan for Saul's life of which Saul was ignorant. God had set Saul apart before his birth "to reveal His Son in [him] so that [he] might preach Him among the Gentiles" (Galatians 1:16). On the road to Damascus, Saul came face to face with the purpose for which God had created him. That encounter changed Saul's life forever. Saul the Pharisee became Paul the Apostle.

Although the encounter with your purpose need not be as dramatic as Saul's was, you too need to discover the purpose for which God created you. I've met many successful people who have been dissatisfied with their accomplishments. They have pursued goals and met them, but they have no fulfillment and continually asked why. Accomplishments without a sense of purpose are meaningless. Life without an understanding of life's purpose leads to disillusionment and emptiness.

A Definition of Purpose

The purpose of something is the reason for which it exists or the manufacturer's original intent for making it. Thus, the purpose of a thing cannot be discovered by asking another thing. Only the manufacturer knows why he created the product the way he did.

God is your Source/Manufacturer. He knows why He gave you life and endowed you with the personality, talents and ambitions that make you unique. He wants you to discover why you were born so you can fulfill your purpose. A sense of purpose gives life meaning. It moves you beyond existence to a fulfilling and productive life.

Change Your Thinking

Jesus had an attitude toward purpose. That attitude is expressed in the words of the Apostle Paul in First Corinthians 2:11:

For who among men knows the thoughts of a man except the man's spirit within him? In the same way, no one knows the thoughts of God except the Spirit of God.

Since you were born separated from God and out of touch with His Spirit, you are ignorant. Jesus pointed to the spiritual ignorance of man when He preached repentance (Matthew 4:17). *Repent* in English primarily means "to regret, or to feel remorse or sorrow for an action, attitude or thought." In the Greek-Roman world of Jesus' day, repentance meant a "change of mind or a turning to God."

Jesus knew that admission into the Kingdom of Heaven required this complete change in thinking. His command to repent initiated God's new work of grace. Many of the religious leaders were offended by Jesus' preaching. They took it as a insult that He would imply that their thinking was wrong.

The truth is, no matter how you are thinking before you meet Jesus, your thinking is wrong. Without God you are ignorant:

So I tell you this, and insist on it in the Lord, that you must no longer live as the Gentiles do, in the futility of their thinking. They are darkened in their understanding and separated from the life of God because of the ignorance that is in them due to the hardening of their hearts (Ephesians 4:17-18).

Without Jesus you cannot come to God:

I am the way and the truth and the life. No one comes to the Father except through Me (John 14:6).

No matter how you are thinking before you meet Jesus, your thinking is wrong.

Life apart from God leads to destruction:

[God] will punish those who do not know God and do not obey the gospel of our Lord Jesus. They will be punished with everlasting destruction and shut from the presence of the Lord and from the majesty of His power... (2 Thessalonians 1:8-9)

God doesn't want you to perish—perish means "to be destroyed":

[The Lord] is patient with you, not wanting anyone to perish, but everyone to come to repentance (2 Peter 3:9b).

Out of His great love and mercy, God provides repentance as the means by which you can avoid destruction. If you don't want to be destroyed by ignorance of God and His purpose for your life, you have to change your way of thinking.

Ignorance of Purpose Leads to Abuse

Ignorance robs you of your potential because it leads to abuse. The word *abuse* is based on two words: *abnormal* and *use.* You can't use something in its natural way unless you know why it exists and how it was designed to be used. Therefore, any time you don't know the purpose of something, you end up using it abnormally, which is abuse.

If you don't know the purpose of a wife, you'll abuse her. If you don't know what a husband is for, you'll abnormally use him. And of course, the greatest tragedy occurs when you don't know what children are for and you abuse them.

Only the Creator Knows the Purpose of a Creation

We must go back to the mind of our Manufacturer to find out the purpose for our existence. Nobody knows the product like the creator, no matter who the creator is. If you make a dress, no one knows that dress better than you. If you build a house, you know where you used old wood that nobody else can see because it's covered by paint.

You are related to where you came from. That means nobody knows you like the One from whom you came. God who created you knows how He designed you to operate. He wants you to understand His thoughts toward you and His purposes for your life. If you try to live without God, you will completely mess up your life, because life without purpose brings abuse.

**If you try to live without God,
you will completely mess up your life,
because life without purpose brings abuse.**

Look around you. Many people have food, houses, cars, friends, mothers, fathers and families that they are abusing.

They don't know the purpose of these people and things so they keep abusing them. If you don't know the purpose of a product, ask its manufacturer. If you don't know the purpose of your family and friends, go to God. Knowledge of purpose is the only way to avoid abuse.

Why Are You Doing What You Are Doing?

First Corinthians chapter thirteen is an example of how we can abuse things if we don't know their purpose. This chapter is often read at weddings because it talks about love. People just love this chapter, but they have a hard time living it. Why? Because they fail to look at the verses that precede it. Chapter thirteen comes out of chapter twelve, which talks about the baptism of the Holy Spirit.

> **There are different kinds of gifts, but the same Spirit. ... Now to each one the manifestation of the Spirit is given for the common good. ... All these are the work of one and the same Spirit, and He gives them to each one, just as He determines. ... And now I will show you the most excellent way. ... Love is patient, love is kind... (1 Corinthians 12:4,7,11,31b; 13:4a)**

If don't have the Holy Spirit in your life, you will abuse love and the one you desire to love. You can't get the result without the living presence of the Holy Spirit in your life. Without Him you will be impatient, unkind, envious, boastful, proud, rude, self-seeking and easily angered in your relationship with your lover. In fact, your love will fail because you don't understand love as an outgrowth of God's power in your life.

Accomplishments Without Purpose Are a Waste of Time

It doesn't matter what you do, if you don't understand why you are doing it you are wasting your time. If you give everything you have to the poor or you sacrifice your body to be burned, but you don't understand the purpose for doing it, all you will have is a dead body (1 Corinthians 13:3). God's not impressed by religious or moral acts unless you know why you are doing them.

Man Without God Is Lost and Confused

Psalm 82 describes man's situation without God:

> **They know nothing, they understand nothing. They walk about in darkness; all the foundations of the earth are shaken. I said, "You are 'gods'; you are all sons of the Most High." But you will die like mere men...** (Psalm 82:5-7a)

We are children of the Most High, but we are living like mere flesh and blood who did not receive the Spirit of God. We are completely without purpose and direction: We don't know anything. We don't understand anything. We (and our world) are totally out of line going nowhere fast. This is the lot of those who do not understand why God created them. Confusion and abuse characterize their lives. You may think God created you to get a good education or to go to church or to make a living. In truth, none of those achieve God's purpose for creating you.

God's Purpose for Man

If you don't know your purpose, it is impossible to fulfill it. Thus the release of your potential requires that you learn why God created you. The Bible clearly defines God's reasons for creating human beings.

Created to Express God's Image

The first chapter of Genesis tells us that God intended for man to express His image:

Then God said, "Let Us make man in Our image..." (Genesis 1:26)

Everything you are is related to your purpose—your height, race, natural talents, gifts and deep desires. God did not create you so you could hate yourself so much that you try to change what you look like. God gave you beauty when He made you. He wants you to look like yourself. Fashionable clothes, cosmetics and hairstyles are fine so long as you know why you are choosing to look like you do. If you just want to look your best or you're trying to make your hair and clothes easier to care for, then go for it. But if you are trying to look like someone else, you're in big trouble. God doesn't want you to look like someone else. He planned that you would be different. He wants you to look like you and act like Him.

God wants you to look like you and act like Him.

Expressing God's image has to do with the way you act, not the way you look. He wants you to mirror His character. He fashioned you so that His *nature* could be revealed through your uniqueness.

The essence of God's nature is succinctly defined in the "love" chapter we looked at earlier. He is the wonderful things this chapter describes.

[God] **is patient,** [God] **is kind.** [He] **does not envy,** [He] **does not boast,** [He] **is not proud.** [God] **is not rude,** [He] **is not self-seeking,** [He] **is not easily angered,** [He] **keeps no record of wrongs. God does not delight in evil but rejoices with the truth.** [God] **always protects, always trusts, always hopes, always perseveres.** [God] **never fails** (1 Corinthians 13:4-8a).

This is how you were created to live. God made you to act like He does. Having God's nature is the difference between *looking* lovely and *being* lovely. One refers to your outward appearance, the other to your nature. You may look good, but be mean. You may dress nicely, but speak unkindly. You may look religious, but act like the devil. God wants you to express His nature. That's one reason He created you.

Created to Enjoy Fellowship With God

God's first question to Adam after Adam's disobedience was "Where are you?" (Genesis 3:9). God had come to the garden in the cool of the day to enjoy fellowship with the man and the woman He had created. The opportunity for fellowship was part of the reason God had created human beings.

Any being that worships or fellowships with God must be spirit. Men and women are the only beings on this planet that God created from His Spirit in His own image. But man lost the fellowship God had designed him to enjoy when he sinned and allowed distance to come between himself and God.

Fellowship is companionship—a mutual sharing of an experience, an activity or an interest. You cannot enjoy fellowship with God unless you have received Jesus as your Savior, because sinful human beings cannot know and understand God's experiences, activities and interests. A reconnection of God's Spirit and your spirit is the prerequisite for the establishment of this companionship. The fulfillment of your purpose to love God and enjoy Him forever is impossible until you reclaim your spiritual heritage, for those who seek to worship God must worship Him in spirit and in truth (John 4:24).

Created to Dominate the Earth

The Genesis description of man's creation includes God's intent that man should have dominion over the earth:

Then God said, "Let Us make man in Our image, in Our likeness, and let them rule over the fish of the sea and the birds of the air, over the livestock, over all the earth, and over all the creatures that move along the ground" (Genesis 1:26).

God created us to dominate the entire earth. But when we lost touch with our Source, we became confused and allowed the earth to dominate us. Every problem that we are experiencing is the result of our not fulfilling our purpose to dominate the earth. We've allowed ourselves to be so dominated by leaves and fruit that they tell us what to do. "It's time for a smoke now. You can't do without me."

But more serious than the domination itself is the deception that goes along with the domination. We are tremendous self-deceivers. Social drinkers say, "I can hold my liquor. I'm not under any pressure to have another drink." But the truth is that every alcoholic started as a social drinker.

When we become dominated by the things we were supposed to dominate, all the earth goes off course. Our world is filled with the violence that revolves around the printed paper that comes from trees. *Money* controls our lives. We kill, rob, steal, cuss and do many other despicable things to get our hands on that sliver of wood.

Even as the domination of people by things destroys our world, so too the domination of people by people creates pain and violence. Husbands abuse their wives. Women abuse their children. Races discrimate against other races. These problems and many more arise from our failure to understand that God gave us dominion over the earth, not over other people.

The lack of knowledge or the loss of insight into the purpose of a person or a thing always leads to confusion and pain. Homosexuality is an excellent example of the resulting turmoil. God created the woman to be a suitable helpmeet to the man. He did not design the male to be a helpmeet to the man or the female to be a helpmeet to the woman. God made them male and female, giving the female to the male. So the purpose of the woman is the man, and the purpose of the man is the woman. Anything else is abnormal use.

The Apostle Paul spoke of this abnormality when he wrote to the church at Rome:

> **The wrath of God is being revealed from heaven against all the godlessness and wickedness of men who suppress the truth by their wickedness... For although they knew God, they neither glorified Him as God nor gave thanks to Him, but their thinking became futile and their foolish hearts were darkened. ... Because of this, God gave them over to shameful lusts. Even their women exchanged natural relations for unnatural ones. In the same way the men also abandoned natural relations with women and were inflamed with lust for one another** (Romans 1:18,21,26-27).

God abhors abnormal use. He destroyed the cities of Sodom and Gomorrah for such evil (Genesis 18-19). Satan, on the other hand, wants you to justify your sin by thinking it is natural. *No amount of rationalizing and spiritualizing can erase the penalties of abuse.* Degradation and corruption wait for those who misuse what God blessed and pronounced as good because "they [receive] in themselves the due penalty for their perversion" (Romans 1:27b). *Twisting the truth to fit your desires does not change the truth, it only opens you further to the father of lies.*

Understanding God's purposes for creating male and female, husband and wife, parent and child is essential for the effective release of your potential and theirs. God created you to dominate the earth. Check your life to see where you are dominating people. Then repent and reestablish those relationships according to God's purposes. Your life depends on it.

Created to Bear Fruit

If you have an apple tree in your backyard that never produces any apples, you're going to get tired of that tree taking up space without bearing any fruit and you'll cut it down. The same is true of God's relationships with people. No tree should ever be without fruit, because God created every tree with its seed inside it. God has a way of moving unproductive people to the side and raising up productive people. *A productive person is simply somebody who will respond to the demand.*

Jesus teaches us in the Gospel of John that God created us to bear fruit:

> **This is My Father's glory, that you bear much fruit, showing yourselves to be My disciples. ... You did not choose Me, but I chose you and appointed you to go and bear fruit—fruit that will last** (John 15:8,16a).

Your fruitfulness is related to the food you are eating. If your spiritual source is not of top quality, your productivity will show it. No matter where you go or what you do, apart from God you will be an ornamental plant without fruit. You are what you eat.

God wants you to reveal all the potential He buried inside you. He offers you tremendous opportunities to share in His work on this earth. Your ability to fulfill God's demand is connected to your relationship with Him because the fruitfulness He desires is the manifestation of His Spirit in your life:

> **But the fruit of the Spirit is love, joy, peace, patience, kindness, goodness, faithfulness, gentleness and self-control. Against such things there is no law. Those who belong to Christ have crucified the sinful nature with its passions and desires. Since we live by the Spirit, let us keep in step with the Spirit** (Galatians 5:22-25).

God created you to bear abundant, life-giving fruit. That's part of your purpose. The presence of the Holy Spirit in your life is the key to fulfilling that purpose.

Created to Reproduce Ourselves

Finally, God created you to multiply and replenish the earth (Genesis 1:28). This ability to have children is sometimes seen as a curse rather than a blessing. Sin is at the root of these feelings.

When God gave Adam and Eve the command to fill the earth, pain was not associated with childbearing. It was not until after sin entered the world that God told the woman:

> **I will greatly increase your pains in childbearing; with pain you will give birth to children. Your desire will be for your husband, and he will rule over you** (Genesis 3:16).

But more important that your ability to physically reproduce is your power to instill in others your values and attitudes. Your life influences your children, your spouse, your friends, your boss, your coworkers, and so on, for good or evil. They watch your actions and hear your words. The effect of your presence in their lives can be either encouraging or discouraging, upbuilding or degrading, postive or negative.

What (or Who) Is Controlling You?

The release of your potential is directly related to your willingness to know, understand and submit to God's purposes for your life. The wisdom and power to accomplish this task is available to all who have the gift of God's indwelling Spirit. For He is the channel through which you can freely communicate with God until your heart and vision become one with His.

The corollary is also true. Life apart from God subjects you to control by other things, people and spirits and conceals the purpose for which you were born. Under those circumstances, you and your potential will be abused. Indeed, much that you have to offer will die with you.

Take time now to examine your life. Who or what is controlling you? Are you releasing your potential by discovering God's purpose for your life?

You have the ability to fulfill that purpose because God built it into you. Determine now to find God's intent for your life.

PRINCIPLES

---

1. Purpose is the creator's original intent for making something.

2. God knows the purpose for your life.

3. Apart from God you are ignorant of your purpose.

4. Ignorance produces abuse.

5. You must understand why you do what you do.

6. You must submit to the control of the Holy Spirit, or something or someone else will control you.

9 Know Your Resources

You can never change the world by being controlled by the earth. All resources should lead to God, their ultimate Source.

Most of us at some point in our lives have wished that we had more resources than we actually have. We have looked at another person's resources and envied them, bemoaning our apparent poverty. This attitude is a stumbling block to releasing our full potential because God's view of poverty and wealth is very different than ours. He is more concerned with what we *do* with what we have, than with how much we *have*.

Poverty and Wealth—A Biblical Viewpoint

Many people believe that God favors the rich and keeps things from the poor, but that is not what the Bible teaches. God loves and cares for all people, rich or poor:

> **The poor man and the oppressor have this in common: The Lord gives sight to the eyes of both** (Proverbs 29:13).

> **Rich and poor have this in common: The Lord is the Maker of them all** (Proverbs 22:2).

Therefore, it is not that God makes rich people and poor people. Rather God makes all people—some who become rich and some who become poor. The key is what you do with the resources God gives you.

Lazy hands make a man poor, but diligent hands bring wealth (Proverbs 10:4).

He who works his land will have abundant food, but he who chases fantasies lacks judgment (Proverbs 12:11).

Do not love sleep or you will grow poor; stay awake and you will have food to spare (Proverbs 20:13).

Poverty is a not a gift from God but the result of your actions. The degree of wealth or poverty in which you find yourself is to a large extent related to the way you are using what you have. A hardworking person becomes rich, while a lazy person becomes poor. Your success is not determined by what you have, but by what you do with what you have.

Your success is not determined by what you have, but by what you do with what you have.

It doesn't matter what your family is like economically. You can decide that you aren't going to stay where your family is. You can resolve to try new things and to work hard. God wants energetic, diligent people. He's always searching for men and women who will look beyond their circumstances to their possibilities.

God's Provisions for All

God created a potent man and supplied him with resources with unlimited potential. Nothing we have today was added to or subtracted from God's original provisions in the garden. But those resources are not equally divided among the peoples of our world. Hardworking, diligent people got their hands on most of the wealth, while lazy, sluggard people watched them take it. Thus, our world knows the rich, the poor and those who are in transit—some gaining wealth and others losing it.

The Effective Use of Resources

When God gives you resources, He wants you to care for them, cultivate them and work them. All of these require effort. An inventor is a thinker who takes his idea and makes it visible. He doesn't create anything new, he just uses his potential to imagine, plan and work so you can see what you were looking at that you didn't know was there. Thus, the people who get ahead in life are those who have learned to understand and use their resources.

Understand Your Resources

Everything has a purpose. Whether or not you work to discover the purpose of your resources determines how effectively or ineffectively you will use them, because understanding must precede use. Use *with* understanding releases potential. Use *without* understanding kills potential. In other words, the proper use of resources maximizes potential, and the abnormal use (abuse) of resources destroys potential.

The proper use of resources maximizes potential, and the abuse of resources destroys potential.

Thus, the release of your potential hinges directly on your ability to know the purpose of your resources, to understand their properties, to obey the laws governing them, and to open yourself to their limitless potential. If you learn what your resources are and how they were designed to operate, you will have limitless potential. But if you use them in an abnormal way, you will destroy your potential.

Cocaine, for example, is used in hospitals to bring healing. But if you misuse it, your thinking will be distorted and you'll end up losing many of the things that are dear to you. Or consider drugs like aspirin and Tylenol, which relieve pain. If you use these drugs according to the directions on the bottle, they have a positive influence. But if you disregard the warning to limit their use, you can kill yourself or make yourself very ill.

Use Your Resources

One of the greatest problems facing the Church is not the *lack* of resources but the *lack of use* of resources. Every resource God gave to Adam is available to us. But we don't use all those resources. Instead of seeing the possibilities in everything God has given us, we categorize our resources and refuse to use some of them because we are threatened by the world's use of them.

What the world is doing or building is not the problem. They don't have any more resources than those they are currently using to solve the world's problems. This is not true for the Church. The Church is not solving the world's problems because we misunderstand the resources that are available to us.

The Bible affirms that all things were made by God, and "without Him nothing was made that has been made" (John 1:3). That means everything belongs to God. The Bible also affirms that "God saw all that He had made, and it was very good" (Genesis 1:31). That means every resource God has given man is good.

The Scriptures are clear that God is the Creator and satan is a perverter. Satan cannot create anything. He can only pervert what God created. Therein lies the source of our problem. Counterfeits abound in our world. They are the result of satan's misuse and abuse of God's resources.

God gives you resources so you can accomplish what He put you here to do. He gives them to you to live *on*, not *for*. When you start living for money you're in trouble. When your job becomes the most important thing in your life, you're in for hard times. Whenever a resource becomes more important than the purpose for which God gave it, you have crossed the line between using it and abusing it.

God gives you resources so you can accomplish what He put you here to do.

Your Available Resources

There are five types of resources you must understand and control if you are going to become a successful person.

Spiritual Resources

First, God has given you spiritual resources. Because God created you in His own image, He gave you the ability to tap into Him.

Man does not live on bread alone, but on every word that comes from the mouth of God (Matthew 4:4).

This spiritual food is available to you in a variety of forms. First and foremost, you must feed your spirit from *the Word of God*:

Blessed are those who hear the word of God and obey it (Luke 11:28).

Stay in a good place where they teach the Word of God. Keep staying there until you get what they are feeding you. You may fall as you learn to walk according to the Spirit, but that's okay. Just pick yourself up and try again. As long as you're feeding yourself spiritual food, you're growing, changing and getting stronger. You may not see that growth, but it's happening whether you see it or not.

The gifts of the Spirit are also resources to feed you:

Now to each one the manifestation of the Spirit is given for the common good (1 Corinthians 12:7).

These resources include the word of wisdom, the word of knowledge, faith, miracles, healings, tongues, interpretation of tongues and prophecy. God gave these wonderful gifts to build up the Church. If you have accepted Jesus as your Lord and Savior, they are available to you.

God also provides *His armor* to protect you:

Therefore put on the full armor of God, so that when the day of evil comes, you may be able to stand your ground, and after you have done everything, to stand. Stand firm then, with the belt of truth buckled around your waist, with the breastplate of righteousness in place, and with your feet fitted with the readiness that comes from the gospel of peace. In addition to all this, take up the shield of faith, with which you can extinguish all the flaming arrows of the evil one. Take the helmet of salvation and the sword of the Spirit, which is the word of God. And pray in the Spirit on all occasions with all kinds of praying and requests (Ephesians 6:13-18a).

Truth, righteousness, peace, faith, salvation, prayer. What wealth! Add to them fasting, giving and forgiving. If your spirit and God's Spirit are in touch, each is yours to use. They can make the difference between a good day and a bad day, between a dismal life and a successful life. Your circumstances may not change as quickly as you'd like, but I guarantee you that your attitudes will.

Physical Resources

Second, God's provisions include physical resources. When God created you, He created your spirit and put it into your body. Because of God's gift of life, your wonderful, physical machine can breathe, move, eat and heal itself. Many of the pleasures you enjoy in life are yours because God took the dust of the ground and fashioned your body. You can see the beauty of flowers, a sunset or a rainbow. You can taste the sweetness of honey or of fruit fresh from the tree. You can feel the love of your children as their little arms encircle your neck and your ears hear those sweetest of words: I love you Mommy. I love you Daddy.

As wondrous as your body is, you may not use it however you desire. Choose carefully the kind of fuel you give your body. Be aware that your body is for food, and food is for your body. Like any of God's resources, improper care and inappropriate attitudes toward your body can result in misuse and abuse:

> "Everything is permissible for me"—but not everything is beneficial. "Everything is permissible for me"—but I will not be mastered by anything. "Food for the stomach and the stomach for food"—but God will destroy them both. The body is not meant for sexual immorality, but for the Lord, and the Lord for the body. ... Do you not know that your bodies are members of Christ Himself? (1 Corinthians 6:12-13,15a)

Material Resources

The third kind of resource God has given you is material resources. God's conversation with Adam in the Garden of Eden shows that God provided well for Adam's needs:

> Then God said, "I give you every seed-bearing plant on the face of the whole earth and every tree that has fruit with seed in it. They will be yours for food" (Genesis 1:29).

The following verses reveal that God also provided gold, aromatic resin, onyx and a river for watering the earth. Indeed, the vast geological and geographical resources of this earth are all part of God's gracious provision for your life.

The Resources of Soul

Fourth, God has supplied you with resources of the soul. Genesis 2:7 tells us that "God formed the man from the dust of the ground and breathed into his nostrils the breath of life, and the man became a living being." You are spirit and you have a soul. The assistance you receive from your mind, your will and your feelings are the resources of the soul that God has given you.

Think what life would be like without these resources. They are the primary means by which you express who you are. Your spirit depends on your soul, as does your body. The Scriptures recognize the importance of the soul:

> **What good will it be for a man if he gains the whole world, yet forfeits his soul? Or what can a man give in exchange for his soul?** (Matthew 16:26)

> **Dear friends, I urge you, as aliens and strangers in the world, to abstain from sinful desires, which war against your soul** (1 Peter 12:11).

> **Dear friend, I pray that you may enjoy good health and that all may go well with you, even as your soul is getting along well** (3 John 2).

Jesus came after the soul because the spirit is easy. It is through your will, your feelings and your mind that satan seeks to attack you. If you guard your soul, your spirit and your body will be well. Their condition depends on the state of your soul. This is clearly revealed in the Bible:

> **For as** [a man] **thinketh in his heart, so is he** (Proverbs 23:7a KJV).

Belief takes place in the spirit, but thinking takes places in the soul. You can believe one thing and think something completely different. What you think is what you become, not what you believe. That's why Jesus came preaching repentance. He knew that our thoughts influence us much more than our beliefs.

> **"The time has come,"** [Jesus] **said. "The kingdom of God is near. Repent** [change your thinking] **and believe the good news!"** (Mark 1:15)

The Apostle Paul explains this further:

> Furthermore, since they did not *think* it worthwhile to retain the knowledge of God, He gave them over to *a depraved mind*, to do what ought not to be done (Romans 1:28).

> The mind of sinful man is death, but the mind controlled by the Spirit is life and peace (Romans 8:6).

> Do not conform any longer to the pattern of this world, but be transformed by the *renewing of your mind*. Then you will be able to test and approve what God's will is—His good, pleasing and perfect will (Romans 12:2).

> For this reason anyone who speaks in a tongue should pray that he may interpret what he says. For if I pray in a tongue, my spirit prays, but my mind is unfruitful. So what shall I do? I will pray with my spirit, but I will also pray with my mind (1 Corinthians 14:13-15a).

The resources of your soul are not available to you unless you allow God to transform your mind.

The Resource of Time

The fifth resource God has given you is *time*. Time is a temporary interruption in eternity. It is a commodity that can be neither bought nor sold. The only thing you can do with time is use it. If you don't use it, you lose it. The Apostle Paul encouraged members of the early Church to "[redeem] the time (Ephesians 5:16 KJV) or "[make] the most of every opportunity" (NIV).

I have discovered that sin is a waste of time. Imagine what you could have done with the hours you spent watching a pornographic video tape, sitting on a bar stool or sniffing that cocaine. You were destroying your mind while you could have been doing something that would teach you or in some way enable you to improve your life.

The only time you have is *now*. Get busy and use it wisely. Say, "God, I am going to use every minute of my day constructively, effectively and efficiently." Time is God's gift—

one of His precious resources. Refuse to be one of those who waste time and then complain because they don't have enough time. Make the hours of your day count.

The only time you have is now.

What Are You Doing With What You Have?

God provides many resources beyond those of spirit, body, material things, soul and time to challenge your potential. How are you using these resources? Or are you even aware that you have these assets?

Perhaps you have a home filled with things that you have worked hard to buy. Do you reserve that house as shelter for your family alone, or do you welcome strangers into its warmth? Do you value the insights of your parents and of others who have lived more years than you? Do you give thanks for your spouse, the helpmeet God has graciously given to you? Or if you are single, do you take advantage of the freedom singleness gives to serve the Lord effectively and wholeheartedly? Are you thankful for your job and the fulfillment and material blessings it affords? Do you recognize that all you own is a blessing from the hand of God, who gives you the means to earn the money to buy the things? Do you willingly share from your resources to meet the needs of others?

The wealth of your resources is limitless if you will allow God to open your eyes to their possibilities. Give from your abundance. Choose wisely when you buy something. *View your resources as gifts to be used in God's service instead of property to be hoarded for your benefit and ease.* Repent (change your thinking) from the "I need more" mentality and use what you already have.

God wants to enlarge your vision of what you have. He wants you to see the storehouses of blessing that presently surround you. Use the anointing God has poured upon the Church and its ministers. Move beyond your shame and let them minister to your needs. Spend time reading God's Word until the Bible becomes for you a treasure of knowledge and inspiration. Go to the library and use the wealth of knowledge accumulated there. Ask questions of your teachers and those who have studied those things you want to know. Read your constitution and take advantage of the freedoms your country offers. Spend time with your children, instilling in them the values you want them to live by and gaining from them a fresh insight into the wonders of life.

You Are Responsible for Your Resources

No matter how rich or poor you are financially, you are accountable to God for the wealth of your resources. *You* have the responsibility to discover, enhance and cultivate the precious gifts you have received from God's hand. The accomplishment of that task begins with the recognition that you are indeed wealthy—perhaps not by this world's standards, but certainly by God's standards. He carefully scrutinizes your attitudes and anxiously watches your use (or abuse) of the resources He has given you.

Determine now to use to the fullest all that God has given you. Refuse to allow the standards and attitudes of this world to influence your efforts to use wisely and effectively the wealth of resources you now own.

For everyone who has will be given more, and he will have an abundance. Whoever does not have, even what he has will be taken from him (Matthew 25:29).

PRINCIPLES

---

1. God makes and provides for all people. Some become rich and some become poor.

2. Wealth and poverty are primarily based on what you do with what you have.

3. God gives you resources to live *on*, not *for*.

4. The proper use of resources releases potential.

5. The improper use (abuse) of resources kills potential.

6. You have many resources that you aren't presently using.

10 Maintain the Right Environment

You are what you eat, and what's eating you.

The story is told of a small boy who wanted to play with his pet fish. So he reached into the fish tank, caught the squirming fish and placed it on the floor beside him. Then he returned to playing with the cars and trucks that were scattered on the floor around him. As he played, he talked to the fish about everything he was doing until he became so engrossed in his toys that he forgot about the fish. Many minutes later, he remembered the fish and turned toward his pet. The fish no longer moved when he touched it. Frightened, the boy ran to his mother with the fish in his hand.

When his mother saw the fish, she quickly took it and put it in the fish tank. The boy watched tearfully as his pet floated on the top of the water. It was dead. When the mother asked her son what had happened to the fish, the boy innocently replied, "Why, we were playing together on the floor when I noticed that he wasn't moving."

Compassionately, the mother replied, "Honey, didn't you know that the fish can't live on the floor? God made fish to live in water."

This story illustrates how much God's creatures depend on the correct environment to live and grow. Even as fish need water to live, so we need the particular environment that God designed for men and women. Too often, however, we are unaware of the impact our environment has on our lives. We flop about like fish on the floor and wonder what's wrong.

God's Care in Setting Ideal Environments

When God created the heavens and the earth, He was very careful to give all that He made an ideal environment. This care is evident, for example, in the earth's placement three planets away from the sun.

The earth's relationship to the sun allows the sun to draw water from the surface of the earth, which then freezes and becomes clouds. When the clouds become heavy, they release the water, which returns to earth as rain. Thus, God's precise positioning of the earth and the sun both affords the earth protection from the sun's radiation and provides the moisture earth's plants and animals need to continue living.

Beware of a Wrong Environment

Violation of environment always produces death. Vegetation that is planted in parched ground will eventually whither and decay. Wildlife that lives in drought areas will die from dehydration and starvation. Fish that live in polluted waters will become sickly and die. The Bible tells a story that illustrates this principle.

Violation of environment always produces death.

Jesus was called to the home of a ruler whose daughter had died. When He entered the house, Jesus found that the professional mourners had arrived and the funeral, with its cacophony of sounds, was in progress. After He had put the noisy crowd outside, Jesus entered the room where the girl lay. In the quietness, He took her by the hand and she got up. The unbelief and mockery of the crowd produced the wrong environment for a resurrection, so Jesus changed the environment.

The Gospel of Mark tells of another occasion when Jesus encountered an environment that obstructed the manifestation of His power:

> When the Sabbath came, [Jesus] began to teach in the synagogue, and many who heard Him were amazed. "Where did this man get these things?" they asked. "What's this wisdom that has been given Him, that He even does miracles..." And they took offense at Him. ... [Unbelief and skepticism so filled the minds of Jesus' friends and neighbors that] He could not do any miracles there, except lay His hands on a few sick people and heal them (Mark 6:2-3,5).

The Gospel of John tells the story of a blind man who was healed by Jesus. When the Pharisees tried to discount the miracle of his restored sight by questioning the integrity and power of the One who had healed him, the blind man refused to be sucked into their attitudes of unbelief.

> Whether He is a sinner or not, I don't know. One thing I do know. I was blind but now I see. ... Nobody has ever heard of opening the eyes of a man born blind. If this man were not from God, He could do nothing (John 9:25,32-33).

Everything Has an Ideal Environment

Everything was designed to function within a specific environment. The conditions of that environment are the specifications that affect the creature's ability to fulfill its purpose. Thus, your potential is directly related to your environment. If your environment is deficient, you will fail to achieve all you were created to do. If your environment is ideal, the possibilities for fulfilling your potential are limitless.

Since an environment consists of the conditions, circumstances and influences that surround and affect the development of an organism, everything that surrounds you or affects your development must be evaluated to see if it is helping or hindering your ability to fulfill your purpose. What happens in your life is determined by who you live with, who you keep company with, where you spend your time and what you feed your mind. The atmosphere on the inside is influenced by the conditions on the outside.

What happens in your life is determined by who you live with, who you keep company with, where you spend your time and what you feed your mind.

This is particularly true of the environment in the home. If you want to function at the maximum of your potential, be careful to establish right relationships with your spouse and your children, and to maintain strong fellowship. The atmosphere of your home must be consistent with the conditions that God originally established for your ideal environment or your potential will be wasted. You can't fix the rest of your life and ignore the conditions in your home.

Study God's Word until you understand the environment He created you to enjoy. Then begin with your home to establish an atmosphere throughout your life in which you can be happy and fruitful. Be especially careful what you feed your mind.

Man's Ideal Environment

God planted a treasure in you. That treasure will never be released unless you learn the conditions of your ideal environment and make the effort to keep your environment in line with those conditions. God set your ideal environment when He created a garden in Eden and put Adam in the garden.

> **Now the Lord God had planted a garden in the east, in Eden; and there He put the man He had formed. And the Lord God made all kinds of trees grow out of the ground–trees that were pleasing to the eye and good for food. In the middle of the garden were the tree of life and the tree of the knowledge of good and evil. A river watering the garden flowed from Eden** (Genesis 2:8-10a).

An examination of the garden's description reveals that:

1. God created the garden;
2. God planted the garden;
3. God organized the garden;
4. God's presence was in the garden; and
5. God provided everything man needed to live in the garden, including faith.

God is at the center of man's ideal environment. That's why life without God is unproductive and unfulfilling. You cannot live outside the environment God designed for you, because you need God's presence. You need a relationship with Him that encourages fellowship and obedience. You need the assurance that He will provide for you and direct your steps. You need the guidance and challenge His laws and commandments provide. Anything less will retard and cancel your ability to develop according to God's plans and purposes.

Life outside the garden does not include these ingredients. Since Adam and Eve's disobedience, we cannot benefit from God's presence and fellowship. Nor can we draw from His creative ability. Our lives are planted in foreign soil that was not planted and organized according to God's intricately designed plans. Chaos and disorganization result when we disobey the laws and commandments

He set for our good. Man is a wreck outside of God's environment.

Man is a wreck outside of God's environment.

The Disruption of the Garden Environment

Our present world is designed to destroy your potential. The minute you leave your house you enter a world that has no interest in your potential. People don't like you and they make you feel like you aren't important. They talk about things that discourage you and attack your values and priorities. This attack on your environment has been around since Adam and Eve experienced similar pressures in the garden.

> **Now the serpent was more crafty than any of the wild animals the Lord God had made. He said to the woman, "Did God really say, 'You must not eat from any tree in the garden'?"** (Genesis 3:1)

Satan's attack came as mental pollution: "Did God really say...?" When the woman repeated what God had said, the serpent went one step farther to devastate the woman's faith in God and His words:

> **"You will not surely die," the serpent said to the woman. "For God knows that when you eat of it your eyes will be opened, and you will be like God, knowing good and evil"** (Genesis 3:4-5).

Thus, the serpent completely undermined the woman's faith in God. The progression of the corruption that controlled Eve also seeks to ensnare you.

Pollution starts with the eyes. Seeing isn't sinning, and looking won't kill you. But if you see, you'll want; if you want, you'll take; and if you take, you'll eat. Thus, seeing is the opening through which sinful thoughts and actions begin to take hold. If you don't want to eat, don't look.

> **When the woman saw that the fruit of the tree was... pleasing to the eye...** (Genesis 3:6)

> **The eye is the lamp of the body. If your eyes are good, your whole body will be full of light. But if your eyes are bad, your whole body will be full of darkness** (Matthew 6:22-23a).

Your trouble deepens when you move from considering the right or wrong of your action to an analysis of the relative merit of what you want. This is particularly true if your good doesn't equal God's good.

> **...the woman saw that the fruit of the tree was good for food...** (Genesis 3:6)

Desire pollutes the environment because it makes you want something at any expense. Your eyes get cloudy and your vision becomes blurred until everything looks right, even though it may be wrong. When desire makes you crave what you want no matter what the consequences, sit tight. You may grab something that will burn you!

> **When the woman saw that the fruit of the tree was...also desirable for gaining wisdom...** (Genesis 3:6)

Sin enters your life when your environment becomes so corrupt that you disobey God's commands and experience the brokenness that follows your disobedience. Suddenly you're in a mess and you're on your own. You no longer have a relationship with God that allows you to rely on His power and wisdom to deal with your problems. That's when your sanity starts to go. That's when pain and heartache fill your days. God doesn't have to convict you of sin because the polluted atmosphere of guilt and excuses will.

When the woman saw that the fruit of the tree was good for food and pleasing to the eye, and also desirable for gaining wisdom, she took some and ate it (Genesis 3:6).

God doesn't have to convict you of sin because the polluted atmosphere of guilt and excuses will.

The Effects of a Wrong Environment

After their banishment from the garden, Adam and Eve entered a world gone awry. The first evidence of this confusion emerges when Cain murders his brother, Abel. Both sons had brought offerings to the Lord, but the Lord looked on Abel and his offering with favor, and on Cain and his offering with disfavor. Cain's anger and jealousy led to disaster as murder entered the world.

Several generations later, we again see the dysfunction that arises from a polluted environment. Lamech, one of Cain's descendants, marries two women (Genesis 4:19) and unfaithfulness enters the world. In the garden God had placed one man with one woman. Outside of the garden, marriage lost its sanctity and men began marrying two wives.

By the time of Noah, the world was so out of control that "the Lord saw how great man's wickedness on the earth had become, and that every inclination of the thoughts of his heart was only evil all the time" (Genesis 6:5). Man's thoughts were so controlled by evil that everything he said and did was wrong. One wrong led to another, which led to another to cover the first, until life became one long string of sinful thoughts and actions. So grieved was God by this situation that He destroyed the earth and all people.

Some time later, men decided to make a name for themselves by building a tower to the heavens (Genesis 11:3-4). Their selfishness further reveals the consequences of a wrong environment. You want everything for yourself with no thought for God or your neighbor.

The evil that characterized the world described in the book of Genesis also plagues our world. A man shoots his wife and children. A woman aborts her child. A teenager jealously stabs another girl to death because of the lost affections of her boyfriend. These horrors and many others reveal our corrupt value system that places little or no worth on human life. They expose the disastrous results of sin and the consequences of our banishment from the garden. Adrift in a world that is riddled with abnormal behavior, we witness and experience a multitude of tragedies.

So overwhelmed is our world by the forces of evil that the love and peace God intended mankind to know have been replaced by hatred, jealousy, immorality and anger. The pain of broken marriages and families has touched us all. The fear and anxiety that make us see even our own flesh and blood as enemies shadows our lives. The consequences of sexual promiscuity stare us in the face. Our environment is out of control and we are powerless to restrain it.

Help in the Midst of Helplessness

Jesus told a story that points to the solution to our messed up environment: A father had two sons. One day not long after he had asked his father for his share of the inheritance, the younger son left home and went to a distant country where he wasted his wealth in wild living. After he had spent everything, he became so hungry that he longed to eat the pigs' food.

> **When he came to his senses, he said, "How many of my father's hired men have food to spare, and here I am starving to death! I will set out and go back to my father and say to him: Father, I have sinned against heaven and against you. I am no longer worthy to be called your son;**

make me like one of your hired men." So he got up and went to his father (Luke 15:17-20a).

What a telling phrase: "When he came to his senses..." It reveals both the son's awareness of his poverty and his belief that his need could be met. He trusted his father's goodness enough to return and ask for forgiveness.

God is well acquainted with the insanity of your world. He offers Himself as the solution to your problems. Through Jesus, He has taken the initiative to restore the garden atmosphere with its gift of His presence, His fellowship and the freedom to obey Him. But He will not force you to accept the new environment that He offers. Like the father of the wayward son, He waits for you to come to your senses and admit your sin and your need of His forgiveness. Only then can He make sense of your world.

God is well acquainted with the insanity of your world.

God dealt with the problem of a polluted environment in Abram's life by asking him to leave everything (Genesis 12:1-4a). Why? Because God knew that Abram's relationship with Him would be compromised by the negative influence of his family and friends.

What's the State of Your Environment?

Take a few moments now to examine your environment. Is it uplifting or degrading? Does it enrich your spiritual life or detract from the work of God's Spirit in your heart? Is obedience to God the norm for those with whom you spend your days or do rebellion and disobedience characterize the lifestyles of your closest friends?

Moses instructed the Israelites to immerse themselves in God's commandments:

These commandments that I give you today are to be upon your hearts. Impress them on your children. Talk about them when you sit at home and when you walk along the road, when you lie down and when you get up. Tie them as symbols on your hands and bind them on your foreheads. Write them on the doorframes of your houses and on your gates (Deuteronomy 6:6-9).

I recommend the same practice to you. For out of a heart centered on God flow His gifts of faith, forgiveness and obedience. These essential ingredients of your God-designed environment testify to a relationship with the Risen Christ that clings to the promise of His presence and delights in the joy of His fellowship. They are the heritage of those who maintain a positive environment so their potential can be released, because a relationship with God always provides the right environment.

A Checklist for Your Environmental Conditions

1. Who are your friends?
2. What books do you read?
3. What movies do you watch?
4. What magazines fill your shelves?
5. What are your hobbies?
6. What are your recreational activities?
7. Who feeds your musical appetites?
8. Who are your heroes?
9. Who feeds you spiritually?
10. Are the conditions of your home, school, work or play conducive to your goals in life?

All the above should be carefully screened, analyzed and adjusted to feed, activate, enhance and foster the release of your potential.

PRINCIPLES

---

1. God designed everything to function in a specific environment.

2. The conditions under which you function properly include:
   the presence of God,
   a relationship with God,
   fellowship with God, and
   the freedom to obey God.

3. Trust, faith, forgiveness and obedience are necessary ingredients of your ideal environment.

4. Keep God's word on your lips to create a positive atmosphere.

5. A wrong environment destroys potential.

6. Leave a wrong environment or change it.

11 | Work: The Master Key

Some dream of worthy accomplishments, while others stay awake and do them.

Jim Michaels, a television journalist in Louisville, Kentucky made the statement in one of his commentaries that "too many workers would rather get home than get ahead." This lack of enthusiasm is clearly evident in the attitudes of many workers who see their jobs as dull, laborious, repetitious, tedious and irritating. Since we spend most of our waking hours working, driving to work or thinking about work, it is no wonder that a depressive attitude characterizes our feelings toward work. Indeed, the only joy many workers get out of their jobs is quitting time.

Although many laborers assume that things are better for high-ranking executives and others with large salaries, those who oversee 500 employees from behind large mahogany desks are not immune to this negative feeling toward work. They too are prone to seeing work as something to be dreaded, like death or taxes.

This attitude toward work has become of great concern to governments, corporations and the media. As major problems with poor quality work, reduced productivity and declining services cripple economic growth, the need and the desire to offer incentives and motivational exercises grow. Thus, aerobics classes, fitness rooms and running tracks have become the focus of much effort and expense in the work place.

Beyond these attempts to improve the vigor and stamina of the average worker, corporate and government leaders are studying the strongest productivity centers of the world. Much of this attention is concentrated on Japan, where the art of work has been mastered since the second world war.

After World War II, Japan was a devastated country. Many of her buildings and people had been obliterated by atomic bombs. She was a pile of rubble. After the war, the United States and other nations helped Japan to rebuild. Computer experts, agricultural specialists, scientists, teachers and business people went to help the Japanese reconstruct their country. They set up manufacturing plants and demanded that the people work for much less than workers in the United States were paid. Because they were so devastated, the Japanese agreed. Today Japan is a power to be reckoned with. Her might is based on economic, not military strength. Her weapon is money.

What Rules Your Life?

No matter how economists and politicians dissect things, the power in our society can be reduced to two basic elements: *God* and *money*. They are the major forces in our world. Jesus warned that we would serve one or the other:

> **No one can serve two masters. Either he will hate the one and love the other, or he will be devoted to the one and despise the other. You cannot serve both God and money** (Matthew 6:24).

Which one you serve has a significant impact on the release of your potential, because the basic power in your life determines what motivates you. If money motivates you, greed will control your actions. If God empowers you, His purposes for your life will control you. The Scriptures promise that God will meet the needs of those who give their first allegiance to Him:

> Therefore I tell you, do not worry about your life, what you will eat or drink; or about your body, what you will wear. Is not life more important than food, and the body more important than clothes? For the pagans run after all these things, and your heavenly Father knows that you need them. But seek first His kingdom and His righteousness, and all these things will be given to you as well (Matthew 6:25-26,32-33).

> My son, do not forget My teachings, but keep My commands in your heart, for they will prolong your life and bring you prosperity (Proverbs 3:1-2).

> The Lord does not let the righteous go hungry... (Proverbs 10:3a)

They also warn that allegiance to money brings trouble and financial bankruptcy:

> Ill-gotten treasures are of no value... (Proverbs 10:2)

> The greedy man brings trouble to his family... (Proverbs 15:27)

> Misfortune pursues the sinner, but prosperity is the reward of the righteous. A good man leaves an inheritance for his children's children, but a sinner's wealth is stored up for the righteous (Proverbs 13:21-22).

This is true because the love of money promotes corrupt morals and perverted values. The need to accumulate more and more material wealth overshadows God's concerns of truth and honesty until deception and dishonesty determine what you do and how you do it.

> The wicked man earns deceptive wages, but he who sows righteousness reaps a sure reward. ... Whoever trusts in his riches will fall, but the righteous will thrive like a green leaf (Proverbs 11:18,28).

The wages of the righteous bring them life, but the income of the wicked brings them punishment (Proverbs 10:16).

This conflict between God and money is very evident in our attitudes toward work.

Do You Work or Go to a Job?

Most of us want jobs, but we don't want to work. We want the money, but we don't want to expend the energy. Nothing is as depressing and frustrating as having someone on a job who's not interested in working. People who want a job without the work are a detriment. They are more interested in being job keepers than workers. They are more concerned with receiving a paycheck than in doing good work.

This attitude is completely contrary to God's concept of work. God wants you to be a good worker, not a good job keeper. He is more interested in your attitude toward work than the status of your checkbook. He has the power to increase your bank account balance, but He can't force you to have a positive attitude toward work.

Our Negative View of Work

Thomas Edison was a great inventor. Many of the things we enjoy today, including the electric light, are the fruit of his willingness to be responsible for the possibilities hidden within him. He was not afraid to roll up his sleeves and work out his potential to make visible that which existed but we couldn't see. His life mirrored his words: "Genius is one percent inspiration and ninety-nine percent perspiration."

"Genius is one percent inspiration and ninety-nine percent perspiration."

Too often we allow the pain and perspiration of work to hide its blessings. We assume that work is a necessary evil without looking for the good it brings. The source of our misconceptions lies in the fact that we equate sin and work. *Although work does not exist because of sin, sin did change the conditions of work.*

> **Cursed is the ground because of you; through *painful* toil you will eat of it all the days of your life. It will produce thorns and thistles for you, and you will eat the plants of the field. By the *sweat* of your brow you will eat your food until you return to the ground, since from it you were taken** (Genesis 3:17b-19a).

Work as God planned it was given to man before sin entered the world. The account of Adam naming the animals precedes the account of Adam and Eve's disobedience. Work as we know it—with its pain, sweat and struggle—reveals the devastation of Adam and Eve's disobedience.

When God told Adam, "Dominate this world I made. Rule this planet," life was new and fresh, and Adam had no knowledge of the power God had built into his brain. So God required Adam to come up with a different name for every animal. As he started naming the birds of the air and the beasts of the field, Adam discovered his potential. Thus, work is a blessing that reveals what you can do. It is the master key to releasing your potential.

Misconceptions About Work

Most of us don't understand the importance of *work*. We prefer rest and relaxation to a good day's *work*. The release of our potential requires that we acknowledge and move beyond the fallacies that characterize our view of work.

Six Days You Shall Labor...

We are a rest-oriented society. We believe that holidays, vacation and weekends are better than work days. This adoration of time free from work reflects our assumption that rest is to be preferred over work. This is a false assumption. Rest is not better than work.

When God created the world, He worked six days and rested one (Genesis 2:2). He also instructed us to work six days and rest one (Exodus 23:12). The result of our desire to work one day and rest six is evident in the boredom and unhappiness that plague our world.

Work always produces more personal growth and satisfaction than rest does. It stirs up your creative abilities and draws from the hidden store of your potential. If you are unfulfilled, you are probably resting too much. You're getting bored because you aren't working. You can't run from work and expect to be happy. Work is the energy that keeps you alive. It's the stuff that gives life meaning. Having six weeks of vacation is not the supreme measure of success or the ultimate prescription for happiness.

**If you are unfulfilled,
you are probably resting too much.**

Retirement Isn't Part of God's Plan

A second fallacy that affects our view of work is the assumption that retirement is the goal of work. You were not designed to retire. You came out of God, and God hasn't retired. He's been working ever since He spoke the invisible into the visible. Therefore, retirement is not part of His plan for your life. Because God created man by giving him an immortal spirit with eternal potential, God planned enough work to keep you busy forever. Oh, you may retire from a specific organization or job, but you can never retire from life and work. *The minute you quit working, you begin to die, because work is a necessary part of life.*

Have you ever met a retired person who was uncomfortable, bitter, rowdy and senile? He became that way because

He retired from work. The lack of work made him crazy because it took away his means of finding fulfillment.

Just like a car runs on gasoline, you run on work. God created you to feel healthy and happy when you are expending energy to reveal all that He put in you. He designed you to find satisfaction in looking at the fruit of your labor. That's why *inactivity often brings depression and discouragement.* God didn't intend for you to sit around and loaf.

God rested when He became tired. He didn't retire. So He says to you, "I'm still working. Why aren't you? There are still things in you that I need." May God deliver you from the spirit of retirement, because retirement is ungodly, unscriptural and unbiblical. Retirement is foreign to God's plan for human beings.

You Can't Get Something for Nothing

A third fallacy that adversely affects your understanding of work is the belief that you can get something for nothing. Nowhere is this fallacy more evident than in our fascination with lotteries. Advertisements for magazine sweepstakes fill our mail boxes. Daily numbers are announced every evening on TV and radio newscasts. Mail order houses promise great wealth if you buy their products. Get-rich-quick schemes, casinos and TV game shows captivate millions and feed them this attitude. The messages of our world encourage our desire to get something for nothing. Sadly, we are taken in by their hype. Until we let go of our hideous attempts to receive benefits without effort, we will forfeit the blessings of work, because work is God's pathway to a satisfying, meaningful existence.

**Work is God's pathway
to a satisfying, meaningful existence.**

You cannot fulfill your purpose without work. Trying to get money by winning the lottery bypasses personal fulfillment.

Neither can you achieve God's intent for your life by reaping the benefits of someone else's efforts. Those who win the lottery often testify that they are more unhappy after they receive all that money than before. Why? Because they lose their reason for getting up in the morning.

Without purpose, life becomes meaningless. Life on "easy street" is not really easy because satisfaction requires effort. In fact, winning a million dollars could very well kill you if you stopped working. Oh, your body might live for a while, but your potential—the real you—would die from lack of use. The joy of life would be gone.

God gives you work to meet your need for personal fulfillment. When you try to get something for nothing you miss the opportunity to find gratification, because effort is the key to satisfaction. Life bears this out in many ways. *Benefits without work short-circuit fulfillment* because you usually have more appreciation for something you worked hard to get. You remember all you went through to obtain it, and from your remembering flows the impetus to treasure and care for the products of your labor. Handouts meet your desire for material possessions, but they deny you the pride of gaining through effort. This is the weakness of a welfare system that robs the individual of the personal responsibility, gratification and pride that comes from self-development and self-deployment.

Work and Responsibility

The only way to rid yourself of the effects of these fallacies is to discover that the love of work is the secret to a productive life. *Without work, you will lose direction and gradually succumb to atrophy.* Your very survival will be threatened as the various facets of your life fall apart from a lack of purpose. So crucial is your need to work that the absence of work is often the issue that underlies problems in interpersonal relationships.

If, for example, a man marries without thinking beyond the pleasures of marriage to the responsibilities of a family, he begins to resent those things that naturally go with marriage and the establishment of a home—things like rent, utility bills, car payments and grocery bills; things like the expenses and obligations that go with children. And, in time, the reasonable responsibilities of a home and a family begin to look unreasonable, and the duties of husband and father become burdens. That's when the problems start, because the man begins to look for a way out of his seemingly intolerable situation. That's when he begins to avoid being at home because he blames his wife and his kids for his multitude of responsibilities. That's when he begins to act irresponsibly by chasing a young lady who doesn't require him to pay the bills or to help meet the demands of family life. In essence, he begins to call responsibility pressure.

Work is God's way to draw out your potential. Through work He opens the door into your inner storehouse and teaches you how to use your talents and abilities to meet the many responsibilities of life. Work and the ability to handle responsibility go hand in hand because work requires you to take on new challenges, dares you to risk failure to show your capacity for success, and prompts you to take the steps to make your dream a reality.

God wants you to fulfill all that He created you to do and be. That's why He is constantly giving you tasks that reveal more and more of the wealth that lies hidden within you. Little by little, He's chipping away at your storehouse of riches, trying to release all that He put in you. But you must cooperate with His efforts. You must refuse to allow the rest/retirement/I-can-get-something-for-nothing mentality to rob you of your need to work. When you accept your responsibility to work and allow God to change your perceptions of work, you will see a difference in your life because God set work as a priority for personal gratification. Work is *the master key* to releasing your potential.

PRINCIPLES

1. God or money will rule your life.

2. An allegiance to money brings physical, financial, social, emotional and spiritual problems.

3. God wants you to be a good worker, not a good job keeper.

4. Work is a blessing that reveals what you can do.

5. Work always produces more personal growth and satisfaction than rest does.

6. Retirement isn't part of God's plan for your life. You will die if you quit working.

7. God gives you work to meet your need for personal fulfillment.

8. Potential needs work to manifest itself.

Potential and the Priority of Work

12

Potential is never realized without work.

Have you ever noticed who God uses? God uses busy people. Truly God loves busy people because their busyness shows that they are willing to work. Jesus' preference for busy people is evident in His choice of four fishermen who were preparing their nets, to be His first followers.

The priority Jesus put on work is also evident later in His ministry as He went through the towns and villages of Galilee and Judea, teaching in the synagogues and healing the sick. He saw there many people who were so helpless and harassed that He likened them to sheep without a shepherd. With compassion, He instructed His disciples to pray for *workers* to meet their needs:

> **Then** [Jesus] **said to His disciples, "The harvest is plentiful but the workers** [laborers] **are few. Ask the Lord of the harvest, therefore, to send workers** [laborers] **into His harvest field"** (Matthew 9:37-38).

Jesus needed *workers*. He needed people who would give their best to bring others into the Kingdom of God. He told His disciples to pray that God would send somebody to work.

God hasn't changed. Work is still a priority for Him. Nor have the needs of our world changed. Helpless, harassed people still need what God stored in us for them.

But we don't appreciate God's ways. We want results without the process. We seek promotion without responsibility. We desire pay without work. You will not participate in the creative power of the One who says, "I've given you the ability to produce. Now work to see what you can do" until you cease to be a reluctant worker. You must stop refusing to work unless someone is standing over you, giving you the work and making sure that you do it. When God commanded Adam to work in the garden, there was no supervisor, manager or time clock to motivate Adam or to force him to work.

God expects us to understand our natural need to work. The Church, and the world at large, must recover God's principle of work because there can be no greatness without work. We must accept the truth that we need to work because God worked and He created us to work.

God Worked

God set the priority of work when He called the invisible world into view. Before there was anything, there was God. Everything we now see existed first in God, but it was invisible. If God had done nothing to get start started, the world we know would not exist. The universe would have stayed inside Him. But God chose to deliver His babies by *working*. He took His potential and, through effort, changed it from potential to experience.

God's efforts in making the world are noteworthy. He determined the number of stars and called them by name (Psalm 147:4). He covered the sky with clouds, supplied the earth with rain and made grass to grow on the hills (Psalm 147:8). He formed the mountains by His power (Psalm 65:6) and set the foundations of the earth (Psalm 104:4). The moon marks the seasons by His decree and the sun sets at the appointed time (Psalm 104:19). So vast and marvelous are God's works in creation that He pronounced them good when He stopped and looked at what He had made. He savored the joy of seeing the wondrous beauty He had brought forth.

> **God saw all that He had made, and it was very good. ... Thus the heavens and the earth were completed in all their vast array. By the seventh day God had finished the work He had been doing** (Genesis 1:31-2:2a).

God didn't create the world by dreaming, wishing or imagining. He created it by *working*. Indeed, God worked so hard that He had to rest.

> **So on the seventh day He rested from all His work. And God blessed the seventh day and made it holy, because on it He rested from all the work of creating that He had done** (Genesis 2:2b-3).

Rest is needed after a long, laborious experience, not a tiny task that requires little effort. God's effort in creation was so extensive that He rested.

Too often we think that coming back to God means we don't have to work anymore. How wrong we are! God loves to work. He delights in pulling new things from His Omnipotent Self. He also requires you to work.

God Created You to Work

After God finished creating the world and planting and organizing the garden, He put Adam in the garden and gave him *work* to do. Indeed, God had work on His mind before He even created human beings.

When the Lord God made the earth and the heavens—
and no shrub of the field had yet appeared on the earth
and no plant of the field had yet sprung up, for the Lord
God had not sent rain on the earth and there was no man
to work the ground, but streams came from the earth and
watered the whole surface of the ground—the Lord God
formed man from the dust of the ground and breathed
into his nostrils the breath of life, and the man became
a living being (Genesis 2:4b-7).

When God created Adam, He gave him dominion over
the fish of the sea, the birds of the air and the living creatures that move on the ground. Although we understand
dominion to be sitting on a throne while others obey our
every command, that is not God's intent. *God equates
dominion with work. Every assignment God gave Adam required work.* The care and protection of the garden required
work. The naming of the animals required work. The subduing of the earth required work. Work was an essential
part of Adam's life.

The same is true for you. God created you to work. He
didn't create you to rest or retire or go on vacation. He
didn't create you to punch a time card or to stand under
the eagle eye of a boss or supervisor. He gave you birth to
experience fulfillment by completing tasks through effort.

**God gave you birth to experience fulfillment
by completing tasks through effort.**

Work is a gift from God. Every assignment God has ever
given required work. Noah worked to build the ark (Genesis
6). Joseph worked to provide for the Egyptians during a
seven-year famine (Genesis 41:41ff). Solomon worked to
build the Temple (2 Chronicles 2-4). As each accomplished
what God asked of him, he fulfilled God's purpose for his

life. His willingness to do the work God gave him blessed himself and others. Through work these people and many others have met the various responsibilities of their lives.

You Need to Work

Work is honorable. God designed you to meet the needs of your life through work. *When you refuse to work, you deny yourself the opportunity to fulfill your purpose*, because God created you to act like He acts, and God worked. The release of your potential demands that you admit that you need *work*.

Work Profits the Worker

All hard work brings a profit... (Proverbs 14:23)

The plans of the diligent lead to profit... (Proverbs 21:5)

...by providing for physical needs.

Make it your ambition to lead a quiet life, to mind your own business and to *work* with your hands...so that your daily life may win the respect of outsiders and so that *you will not be dependent on anybody* (1 Thessalonians 4:11-12).

Work profits the worker by allowing him to meet his *financial responsibilities*. The Apostle Paul provided for his own needs by making tents (1 Thessalonians 2:6-9). He did not rely on the provisions of others, but whenever possible, worked for his living.

The same is required of you. Don't become a burden on others. Work to provide for yourself and your family. Settle down and get a job. Put your roots down and do not allow yourself to be easily deterred from your responsibilities. God gave you work to earn the bread you eat.

...by revealing potential.

God also ordained that work would show you your potential. Although all work brings profit, the reward is not always a financial one. You may feel like you are working hard but you're not getting paid what you are worth. Keep working so you can reap the profits of your work. God does not lie. Even if no one ever pays you, your work profits you because you discover what you can do. It is better to deserve an honor and not receive it than to receive an honor and not deserve it.

...by unveiling the blessings of work.

Work is much more important than honor because it brings the learning that releases your talents, abilities and capabilities. It is also more valuable than a paycheck. When you stop working for money, you'll discover the blessing of work.

The laborer's appetite works for him; his hunger drives him on (Proverbs 16:26).

...by giving the opportunity to rejoice in achievement.

A commitment to work will also permit you to develop a perspective that rejoices in achievement more than pay. Then you can find happiness in your work even when the pay is less than what you expect or deserve. Administrators give those who are busy more to do because they know the busy people are willing to work. *If you want to be promoted, get busy. Become productive.* Refuse to live for coffee breaks, lunch hours and quitting time. Take your tasks and do them well. When you work, work because you want to know what you can do, not because you are trying to get paid. You may not be noticed immediately, but your promotion will come. Excellent work always profits the worker.

...by building self-esteem.

Finally, work profits you by enhancing your self-esteem. If you feel worthless, find some work. Get busy. When you have something to do, your ability to feel good about yourself can change overnight. As you take the opportunity to focus on the results of your labor instead of the losses in your life that tempt you to feel unloveable and incapable, your estimation of yourself will grow. Work keeps you healthy, physically and emotionally.

Work Blesses Others

Share with God's people who are in need. Practice hospitality (Romans 12:13).

Work affords the opportunity to help others. Indeed, the Gospel of Matthew records a parable in which our willingness to help meet the needs of others is the basis on which our faithfulness or unfaithfulness to Christ is judged (Matthew 25:31-46). The Apostle Paul notes the benefits of sharing when he commends the Corinthian church for their willingness to help sister churches in need (2 Corinthians 8-9). He advises them to give generously not grudgingly, with the promise that what they give and more will be returned to them:

Remember this: Whoever sows sparingly will also reap sparingly, and whoever sows generously will also reap generously. Each man should give what he has decided in his heart to give, not reluctantly or under compulsion, for God loves a cheerful giver. ... Now He who supplies seed to the sower and bread for food will also supply and increase your store of seed and will enlarge the harvest of your righteousness. *You will be made rich in every way so that you can be generous on every occasion...* (2 Corinthians 9:6-7,10-11a)

So Who's Stealing?

If I were to ask you to describe a thief, you would probably talk about someone who entered your home and took your possessions. This is certainly a legitimate definition, but the thief doesn't always have to sneak in and out to take what isn't his.

Many of us go to work and steal from our bosses. We come to work late, take extra long lunches hours and go home early. Or we take home the pencils, paper, pens and paper clips that belong to the company, we make private copies on the boss's copy machine and we conduct personal business on company time. These actions are no better than those of a thief who enters your home and takes your possessions because both result in the loss of goods that someone else worked to provide.

In an even broader sense, a thief is anyone who relies on the productiveness of another to provide for his needs because he is too lazy to meet them himself. If you are able to work and you're not working, you are stealing from those who are working. You're requiring them to provide what you could get for yourself if you would work. If you are eating but not working, or you are living in a house but not working, you are a thief. *Taking the benefits of work without participating in the effort is theft.*

If you are able to work and you're not working, you are stealing from those who are working.

Thus, a son who plays baseball all day then comes in and messes up the house his mother spent all day cleaning is a thief. He has stolen her energy. Likewise, an adult child who is out of school, but lives at home, steals from his parents if he goes into the kitchen and eats from the pot that is on the stove without helping to provide what's in the pot.

Theft goes even farther than relying on another's effort. You are pregnant with babies that need to be born. You have talents, abilities and capabilities that God wants you to share with the world. But you will never see them unless you begin to understand God's definition of work and His purpose for giving you the opportunity to share His creative powers. Your potential is dying while you are sitting around doing nothing.

If you steal something, you don't stop and look at it. Instead of admiring your efforts, you worry about who's going to take your things from you. Or you are so busy seeing how little work you can do without being caught that you have accomplished nothing at the end of the day that merits the pride of accomplishment. *The absence of work is stealing. Likewise, the cure for stealing is work–doing something useful with your hands.*

> He who has been *stealing* must steal no longer, but must work, doing something *useful* with his own hands...
> (Ephesians 4:28)

Usefulness is more than a job. It's making a profitable contribution to the world. It's gaining so you can give. It's finding wholesome, legal work that helps and blesses another, instead of immoral degrading behavior that harms and destroys. Usefulness recognizes the accomplishments of others and tries to complement them.

The Penalities of Laziness

Sitting around is no more acceptable to God than taking what does not belong to you. You rob yourself and others when you are lazy. Like any theft, laziness carries many penalties. The first of these is *hunger*:

> The sluggard craves and gets nothing, but the desires of the *diligent* are fully satisfied (Proverbs 13:4).

> Laziness brings on deep sleep, and the shiftless man goes hungry (Proverbs 19:3).

Even when we were with you, we gave you this rule: "If a man will not work, he shall not eat" (2 Thessalonians 3:10).

A second penality of laziness is *isolation* and *shame*:

In the name of the Lord Jesus Christ, we command you, brothers, to keep away from every brother who is idle... Do not associate with him, in order that he may feel ashamed (2 Thessalonians 3:6).

A poor man is shunned by all his relatives—how much more do his friends avoid him! (Proverbs 19:7)

A third penalty of laziness is *others' reluctance to take you seriously*, because lazy people always have an excuse why they aren't working.

The sluggard says, "There is a lion outside!" or, "I will be murdered in the streets!" (Proverbs 22:13)

A fourth penalty of laziness is *lost opportunities for advancement* because jealousy and overconcern for the progress of others prevents you from doing your work.

Do you see a man skilled in his work? He will serve before kings; he will not serve before obscure men (Proverbs 22:29).

Be sure you know the condition of your flocks, give careful attention to your herd; for riches do not endure forever and a crown is not secure for all generations (Proverbs 27:23-24).

A fifth penalty of laziness is *the inability to see your own need to get up and work*:

The sluggard is wiser in his own eyes than seven men who answer discreetly (Proverbs 26:13).

A sixth penalty of laziness is an increasing *loss of ambition*:

The sluggard buries his hand in the dish; he is too lazy to bring it back to his mouth (Proverbs 26:16).

Go to the ant, you sluggard; consider its ways and be wise! It has no commander, no overseer or ruler, yet it stores its provisions in summer and gathers it food at harvest (Proverbs 6:6-7).

A seventh penalty of laziness is *the desire to sleep*:

As a door turns on its hinges, so a sluggard turns on his bed (Proverbs 26:15).

An eighth penalty of laziness is *the inability to take pride in what you have accomplished* because you haven't accomplished anything.

The lazy man does not roast his game, but the diligent man prizes his possession (Proverbs 12:27).

A ninth penalty of laziness is *slavery*:

Diligent hands will rule, but laziness ends in slave labor (Proverbs 12:24).

An tenth penalty of laziness, and the most severe, is *poverty*. Poverty is the cumulative result of all the other penalities.

All hard work brings a profit, but mere talk leads only to poverty (Proverbs 14:23).

How long will you lie there, you sluggard? When will you get up from your sleep? A little sleep, a little slumber, a little folding of the hands to rest—and poverty will come

on you like a bandit and scarcity like an armed man
(Proverbs 6:10-11).

Lazy hands make a man poor... (Proverbs 10:4)

A sluggard is a lazy bum—my mother used to call them
"grassy bellies." When I was young I didn't understand what
my mom meant. But one day when I was sitting in the library
at the university I realized that Mom called sluggards grassy
bellies because they lay on their bellies long enough for
grass to grow on them. The Greek word for *poor*, as used
by Jesus, is *poucos,* which means "nonproductivity." That's
what poverty is. To be poor doesn't mean you don't *have*
anything. It means you aren't *doing* anything.

Poverty is cured by hard work. If you don't work you will
end up begging. Or you'll become a slave to your boss because you refuse to work for your own satisfaction in completing the job and wait for him to force you to work.

Poverty is cured by hard work.

Look at the birds. God provides food for them, but they
have to go and look for it. They have to dig and pull it out
of the ground. So it is with you. God has given you many
talents and ambitions to bring satisfaction and fulfillment
into your life. But you have to go and look for that fulfillment. You can't sit back and wait for it to come to you,
because it will never come. Work is God's path to an abundant, fulfilling life that reveals the wealth of your potential.
*God established your need to work when He worked out His
potential in creation and demanded the same of Adam.*

PRINCIPLES

1. God worked, and He created you to work.

2. Subduing and dominating the earth requires work.

3. When you refuse to work, you deny yourself the opportunity to fulfill your potential.

4. The absence of work is stealing.

5. You rob yourself and others when you are lazy.

6. Poverty is cured by hard work.

13 | Understanding Work

Working for fulfillment is better than working for money. The purpose of a job is work, not money.

A study of history reveals that all great empires were built on the sweat and blood of a labor force, whether the energy of the workers was given voluntarily or through force. The civilizations of Egypt, Greece, Rome and Assyria were built on the backs of subjugated peoples. The United States was built on slavery. No matter how the workers are motivated, there must be work to achieve greatness.

The power of productivity is evident today in the influence of labor unions. Because unions control the workers, who control the productivity, they can cripple a country, destroy an economy and control a government. And once you control productivity, you control wealth.

Do you know how countries measure their strength and wealth? They measure it not by the money they have in their treasury, but by their GNP, which means Gross National Product. Thus, the relative strength or weakness of a country is measured by the level of employment and productivity. The power of productivity is work. You can't run a country where the people aren't working because you can't force people to work. Governments can't legislate obedience, nor can they force people to cooperate without question. Everybody has rights, a will and a conscience. Sooner or later, workers will rebel if they feel they are working for nothing. Out of sheer desperation they will try to control their own destiny. There's power in work—much more power than churches, governments or other social organizations have—because the workers control productivity and, therefore, the destiny of the nation.

The story of Moses and the Pharaoh of Egypt illustrates this truth. Pharaoh wasn't threatened by the person of Moses, or even by the God of the Israelites. He was threatened by the loss of a major work force. Thus, when Moses proposed a three-day journey into the desert to offer sacrifices to God, the king of Egypt replied:

"Moses and Aaron, why are you taking the people away from their labor? Get back to your work! ... Look, the people of the land are now numerous, and you are stopping them from working." That same day Pharaoh gave this order to the slave drivers and foremen in charge of people: "You are no longer to supply the people with straw for making bricks... They are lazy; that is why they are crying out, 'Let us go and sacrifice to our God.' Make the work harder for the men so that they keep working and pay no attention to lies" (Exodus 5:4-9).

When people decide they aren't going to work, the back of a nation is broken. We have seen this in the recent past as the former Soviet Union and other countries have changed dramatically through the power of the worker. Thus, the demise of world-class companies is not the fault of the board or the president. The cause rests with the little guys who push wheels on a plane or weld car parts together. Our countries are falling apart because our people are refusing to work, and work well. We must change our attitudes toward work. Our only hope is to rediscover God's definition of work and the benefits He intends work to bring to our lives.

God's Definition of Work

Our definition of work and God's are very different. Work is not the same as a job. Work releases potential; a job provides a paycheck. While you may work at your job, work does not always result in a financial reward. Work arises out of a desire to contribute to the world's wealth and well-being by giving of yourself. It moves beyond effort under the force of another and avoids the "I'm not going to work because you can't make me work" mentality.

**Work releases potential;
a job provides a paycheck.**

Frequently we make work overly sophisticated. We need to get labor back into work. We need to *labor* in the office, not just *go* to the office. God didn't say, "Six days you shall go to your job," but "six days you shall work." Until we change our attitude toward work we will not obey this commandment.

Labor isn't so much *doing things* as *delivering hidden stuff*. It's delivering the babies you will die with if you don't work them into sight. It doesn't matter what kind of job you have, whether you are an executive, a salesman, a factory worker or a housewife. Work as though your life depended on it, because it does.

Jesus commanded us to pray for *laborers*. This term is also used to describe the process of a woman in childbearing. The process of delivering the pride and joy of a new baby—the hidden potential—involves conception, time, development, adjustments, labor, pain and cooperation. All are necessary for the manifestion of a child. This process is the same for all humanity. Labor delivers!

Work is God's way of revealing your talents, abilities and capabilities. It helps you to discover the satisfaction of accomplishment and the results of perseverance. Without work you'll never see the results of your potential. Without effort you'll never feel the satisfaction of accomplishment.

Work is activated strength and energy.

Jesus worked while He was on the earth. He gave sight to the blind and hearing to the deaf. He caused the lame to walk and the leper to be clean. He preached the good news of God's coming Kingdom and welcomed sinners into God's family. Again and again He called on His strength and energy to meet the demands of lonely, harried, fearful, needy people. Had He chosen to withhold the potential He possessed to better the lives of those He met, His power would have remained hidden and His purpose would have been lost. But Jesus knew that He had been sent to redeem a suffering, dying world. He accepted the task God gave Him and worked to change the course of history. Indeed, the results of His work were the clues Jesus pointed to when He was questioned whether He was the One to be sent from God.

> Jesus said to them, "My Father is always at His work to this very day, and I, too, am working" (John 5:17).

You have a similar responsibility to release the strength and energy God gave you for the good of the world. You can accomplish this through work. The Greek word *ergon*, which means "to activate," is often translated *work*. From *ergon* comes our word "energy." Thus, work is the activation of stored energy. If a car is parked, it is inoperative. But the minute you start the engine, the pistons begin working and the car has the power to move. Work is the God-given method that empowers you to operate. Through work you can do and become all that God intended for your life.

This concept of becoming is further clarified in another Greek word for work, *energia*, which means "to become." No matter what God requires of you, if you don't do it, you can't become what He sees in you. *Potential is the existence of possibilities. Work is the activation of possibilities.* Potential without work remains potential—untapped, untouched, untested!

God created you to be a genius. He endowed you with enough thoughts, ideas and desires to fulfill every expectation He has for your life. But the presence of potential does not make you a genius. You are not *born* a genius. You *become* one by working to release what you have. Geniuses are people who work relentlessly to accomplish what they believe can be done. They try again and again until they receive in the physical what they see in their imaginations. They activate their hidden strength and energy to become what they are and to accomplish what they already possess. Geniuses use God's gift of work to achieve what no one else has done. God planned for you to be a genius. Remember, "Genius is one percent *inspiration*, and ninety-nine percent *perspiration*."

Potential is what you have. Work is what you do. What you do with what you have makes the difference between a life of strength and energy, and a life of weakness and defeat. God gives you work to activate your power. Through work you become what you are.

Through work you become what you are.

Work is bringing something to pass.

A fantasy is a dream without labor. It is also a vision without a mission. When God gives the potential for something, He also demands that it be worked out. The story of Abraham is a good example of this principle.

One day when God and Abraham were on top of a mountain, God told Abraham that He would *give* him everything as far as he could see to the north, south, east and west. Then God told him to *walk* the length and breadth of the land to *receive* what he had been promised (Genesis

13:14-17). Along with the promise came the command to work. Before Abraham could take possession of his inheritance, he had to fight those who lived in the land. The promise would not be possession without effort.

The same is true for you. Every time God gives you a promise, He also gives you the command to work to receive what He has promised. God doesn't just deliver like Santa Claus. You have to fight to get what is yours. The potential to possess what God has given is within you, but you will not obtain the promise until you put forth the effort to claim it.

So if you need money to pay your bills, don't wait for someone to drop the dollars into your hand. Get up and take the job God sends.

Every job, no matter how much you dislike it, is working for you. If you can educate yourself to work no matter what the conditions are, you will learn discipline, because the work is more important than the conditions. Work is also more important than the job. If a child always gets what he wants, he learns to expect his wants to be met without any effort on his part. Our world is full of adults who act like spoiled children. They never learned the value of work.

We do well when we learn the lesson early in life that God requires us to work for what we want. One of the greatest things parents can do for their children is to demand that they learn the responsibility of work at an early age. If your child has to work for his spending money, he will soon learn that he can't get something for nothing. *Work brings potential to pass.* Without work, all you have is potential.

Work is using your abilities and faculties to do or perform something.

When God wanted a place to live, He could have created a magnificent dwelling by speaking it into place. But He chose to have man build the house for Him. Thus, God instructed Moses to gather offerings for the Tabernacle and to employ skilled craftsmen to create its various parts. After Moses had collected the materials and the workers, the work began. Silversmiths, goldsmiths, carpenters, glass cutters, weavers, embroiderers and gem cutters all contributed their *skills* until the dwelling place of God was completed. Then the Lord, through His presence in the cloud by day and the pillar of fire by night, entered and filled the Tabernacle *they had prepared.*

God has given you a wealth of skills, talents and abilities. Work is the means to discovering those resources. Persistent, consistent effort polishes the gems within you, making your life a suitable dwelling place for our holy God. It activates your potential and enables you to share your expertise and proficiency. The release of your gifts will benefit the world for generations to come.

Work is the means to produce a desired result.

When the Israelites returned from exile in Babylon, Nehemiah, the governor of Jerusalem, led the people in repairing the walls of the city. Because he had a burden to repair the gates destroyed by fire and to rebuild the buildings that lay in rubble, he toured the ruins and asked the officials of Jerusalem to work with him. When scoffers ridiculed them, Nehemiah replied, "The God of heaven will give us success" (Nehemiah 2:20). He believed that the dream was from God and, therefore, trusted Him for the attainment of his goal. His efforts were aided by those who "worked with all their heart" (Nehemiah 4:6). Time and again God frustrated the plots of those who would have threatened Nehemiah's dream, thus proving that He will fight for those who undertake to fulfill His purposes.

Work coupled with a mind to do what God desired brought victory for the Israelites who were commited to the rebuilding of the wall of Jerusalem. *Commited work toward a desired result is also a key to your success.*

Potential and the Benefits of Work

Work provides the means through which the knowledge you gained through the study of the other keys can be activated. It takes you from knowing that you must live by faith to acting on what you know. The same is true for your, purpose, resources and environment. Knowledge is not profitable until it is translated into action. Work is the translator God has provided.

Work gives flesh to faith.

God has given you many dreams. He's planted seeds in your imagination and supplied you with goals you'd like to meet. Indeed, you may be pregnant with answers to some of the world's great problems. If you are going to realize those dreams, you'd better be ready to work. Until you start working, your power to benefit mankind will remain untapped.

Until you start working, your power to benefit mankind will remain untapped.

A fantasy is a dream without work. It is also a vision without a mission. You can have all the vision you want, but until you get a mission, your vision will be no more than a wishful thought. I love missionaries because they are willing to take the vision and make it a reality. Visionaries, on the other hand, disturb me because they are not willing to put forth the effort to accomplish their dreams. If you don't work, you are fantasizing. You are wasting your time on worthless ideas. Work is the means to make what you see into what you receive. Visionaries must become missionaries to be effective and successful.

Work provides the opportunities to fulfill purpose.

Work is part of your design. If you're not working, you're not fulfilling your purpose. Most of the people who are burdens on society—those who are on welfare or receive some other social services—are not part of the work force. The food stamps, medical assistance and rent assistance they receive come from the pockets of those who work and pay taxes. Thus, everyone who asks the government to pay their bills is living out of your pocket if you are working. Those who live on welfare are deficits to the country.

In God's system, everyone *needs* to work. *You* need to work. Your ability to dominate and subdue the earth is related to the effort you put forth to accomplish the tasks God gives you. If you refuse to work, your potential to express God's image and to bear fruit are sealed inside you, dormant and useless. Without labor there is no fruit and the blessings God wants to give you are forfeited. Your refusal to work destroys the possibilities you possess to cooperate with God's work of creation.

Work expands your resources.

It's not how many resources you have but how much work you generate with those resources that will control your poverty or wealth. Potential without work is poverty because your willingness to work is the key to the realization of your potential. The real question isn't how much potential you have but how much potential you will work to show. Everybody has potential—which is dormant ability, hidden strength, untapped strength and unused resources—but not everybody works to release what they have.

Work is crucial to the care and multiplication of your resources. If you are faithful over little, God will make you ruler over much. But He can only give as much as you are willing to accept. Faithfulness over little things brings larger responsibilities and more work, which brings more resources and larger responsibilities and so on. Well done is always better than well said. Work is the means to multiply what God has already entrusted into your care, be it great or small.

Work releases and maintains your environment.

People tend to gravitate to those who think and act like they do. This is certainly true of those who avoid work. Lazy people don't like to be in the company of diligent people because their nonproductivity is readily visible.

Thus, work is the key to establishing a positive environment. Your devotion and persistence in accomplishing the tasks of job, church, family, etc. will attract the company of others who like to work. Likewise, idleness will draw to your side people who are not interested in working. If you choose to be lazy, the penalties of laziness will overcome you as you become ensnared by a crowd that scorns effort and diligence. The very environment that snuffed out your desire to work in the first place will continue to stunt your development. Devote yourself to work and avoid all who do not share your devotion. The company you share will soon reflect and encourage your desire to work.

How to Work Out Your Potential

Are you hungry to accomplish something? Are you so committed to a vision that you will do anything to see that vision come to life? Then make plans and follow them.

> **The plans of the diligent lead to profit as surely as haste leads to poverty** (Proverbs 21:5).

There's a difference between plans and haste. Haste is trying to get something for nothing. Haste leads to poverty. But the hard worker make plans and expends the effort to see those plans pay off.

Do you want to be a lawyer, a doctor, a teacher, a carpenter, a policeman, a minister, a secretary, an accountant or a politician? Put some work behind that dream. Burn the midnight oil and study. Make the acquaintance of a person who is working in your chosen field and work with him to learn the trade, business or profession. The completion of your plans is related to your willing to work, as is your prosperity. Likewise, *the release of your potential is dependent upon your expenditure of the necessary effort to change your thoughts into visible realities. Work of your own intiative. Don't wait for life to force you to work.*

Work is the key to your personal progress, productivity and fulfillment. Without work you can accomplish nothing. God assigns you work so you can release your possibilities and abilities by putting forth the effort to accomplish each task. A pessimistic attitude toward work breeds dissatisfaction and unhappiness. A healthy perspective builds self-esteem and nurtures a positive, confident outlook on life. The responsibilities God gives you are presented to provoke your potential and to challenge you to try new things. Until you stop being a reluctant worker you will miss the vitality and meaning that God intended work to bring to your life.

Work is the key to your personal progress, productivity and fulfillment.

Accept today God's gracious gift of work. Refuse to allow a pessimistic attitude toward work to rob you of your potential. Then look forward to the joy of accomplishment and the delight of discovering all God put in you for the world. You will truly find that work is a blessing.

PRINCIPLES

---

1. The achievement of greatness requires work.

2. Labor delivers your potential.

3. Work is...
   activated strength and energy,
   the effort required to bring something to pass,
   the use of your abilities and faculties to do or perform something, and
   the means to produce a desired result.

4. Faith without work is unproductive.

5. God designed you to fulfill your purpose by working.

6. Work multiplies your resources, be they large or small.

7. Idleness invites the company of lazy people.

8. The release of your potential is dependent upon your expenditure of the necessary effort to change your thoughts into visible realities.

14 Responding to Responsibility

The greatest need of ability is responsibility.

One of the most beautiful sounds to ever enter the human ear is the first cry of a newborn baby—*the sound of life*! Millions of people over the years have experienced much joy, elation, celebration and relief at this sound. Yet, a newborn's cry also signals the arrival of responsibility. Not only do the parents have the responsibility for the new infant but the child himself becomes accountable for the awesome potential he possesses at birth.

Responsibility is defined as a state of being reliable, dependable, accountable, answerable and trustworthy. Responsibility also involves entering into a contract or an obligation. All of these indicate the transfer of something valuable, with the implication that the receiver of the trust is to achieve some positive result. Responsibility also embraces self-reliance, effectiveness, faithfulness and capability. In essence, responsibility is simply *the ability to respond*.

All human beings come to this world pregnant with potential. Each person, like a computer, has a tremendous capacity to compute, analyze, assimilate, compare and produce. But this ability is useless until it is programmed and demands are made on it. Your potential, ability and natural talent were given by divine providence for the purpose of preparing the next generation to fulfill its potential. No one comes to this earth empty. Everyone comes with something. Just like a seed has a forest within it, so you have much more than was evident at your birth.

Unlike the seed, however, you are not dependent on a farmer to plant and cultivate your potential. You are accountable for the time you spend on this planet. The responsibility for activating, releasing and maximizing this hidden, dormant ability is yours alone. The fact that you were born is evidence that you possess something that can benefit the world. No matter what you have done or accomplished, there is still much more inside you that needs to be released. Only you can release it.

**You are accountable for the time
you spend on this planet.**

I am convinced that life was designed to create environments that make demands on our potential. Without these demands our potential would lie dormant. This thought is reflected in the saying, "Necessity is the mother of invention." How true! Most of us respond to life creatively and innovatively only when circumstances *demand* that response. The many technological, medical and social breakthroughs that have been achieved because problems or circumstances demanded a response vividly illustrate this truth. The book of Genesis also clearly reveals this principle in the account of man's first encounter with creation in the Garden of Eden.

Man, as God first created him, was one hundred percent unreleased potential. He was an adult with full capabilities, talents and gifts. His physical, mental, intellectual, emotional and spiritual powers were fully developed. But man's powers and abilities were totally unused, untapped, unmanifested, unchallenged and unemployed. The Creator's plan for releasing this hidden ability is recorded in Genesis 2:15,19-20:

> The Lord God took the man and put him in the Garden of Eden to *work* it and *take care* of it... Now the Lord God had formed out of the ground all the beasts of the field and all the birds of the air. He brought them to man to see what he would call them; and whatever the man called each living creature, that was its name. So the man gave names to all the livestock, the birds of the air and all the beasts of the field.

God's first action after creating this totally new man—a man with muscles that had never been exercised, a brain that had never been stimulated, emotions that had never been aroused, an imagination that had never been ignited and creativity that had never been explored—was to give him assignments that placed demands on his hidden abilities. By giving Adam's ability responsibility, God placed demands on Adam's potential. In a similar manner, your potential is released when demands to fulfill an assignment in God's greater purpose for your life are placed on you. This is why *work* is called *employment*—it employs your abilities for the purpose of manifesting your potential.

God's command to *work* required Adam to use his physical potential. Likewise, God's commands to *cultivate the garden* and to *name the animals* activated his intellectual, mental and creative potential. The demands God makes on you accomplish the same thing in your life. The release of your potential demands that you accept the responsibility to work, because the greatest need of ability is responsibility. You will never know the extent of your potential until you give it something to do. The greatest tragedy in your life will not be your death, but what dies with you at death. What a shame to waste what God gave you to use.

You will never know the extent of your potential until you give it something to do.

Dying Empty

Have you ever noticed the deep peace and contentment that come over you when you fulfill a responsibility? Nothing is more rewarding and personally satisfying than the successful completion of an assigned task. The joy and elation that fill you at such times are the fruit of achievement. The experience of fulfillment is directly related to this principle of *finishing*.

An old Chinese proverb says: "The end of a thing is greater than its beginning." In other words, finishing is more important than starting. The beginning of a task may bring a degree of anxiety and apprehension, but the completing of a task usually yields a sense of relief, joy and fulfillment.

Finishing is more important than starting.

History is filled with great starters who died unfinished. In fact, the majority of the five billion human beings who inhabit the earth will die unfinished. What a tragedy! What counts is not how much a person starts, but how much he or she finishes. The race is not to the swift, but to him that endures to the end.

Jesus finished His task on earth. The words He spoke on the cross clearly indicate that He fulfilled an assignment, completed a task and satisfied a requirement. They resonate with a deep sense of peace. In fact, they confirm that He was not killed but simply *died*.

> **When He had received the drink, Jesus said, "It is finished." With that He bowed His head and gave up the ghost** (John 19:30).

Because He had released and maximized His potential to successfully fulfill the purpose for which God had sent Him into the world, Jesus saw death not as something to be feared, but as the natural next step. In other words, Jesus went to the grave empty.

This principle of *finishing* is also expressed very clearly by the Apostle Paul in his second letter to Timothy:

> **For I am already being poured out like a drink offering, and the time has come for my departure. I have fought a good fight, I have finished my race, I have kept the faith** (2 Timothy 4:6-7).

Paul faced death with complete confidence and peace because he knew that he had fulfilled God's purpose for his life. When he spoke of being "poured out," which suggests emptying some contents from oneself, he pointed to an accurate and important concept that must be understood by all who would release their potential.

You, like Paul and our Lord Jesus Christ, were born for a purpose. The ability to fulfill that purpose resides deep inside you screaming to be released. Perhaps you yearn to write books, compose songs, scribe poetry, obtain an academic degree, paint on canvas, play music, open a business, serve in a political, civic or spiritual organization, visit other countries or develop an invention. Think how long you've carried your dream. Recall how many times you have postponed satisfying your desire. Count the many times you began to realize your goal only to quit.

God did not intend that the cemetery would be the resting place of your potential. The grave irresponsibility of taking your precious dreams, visions, ideas and plans to the grave is not part of His design. You have a responsibility to release your potential. Join Jesus, Paul and many others who robbed death of the pleasure of aborting their potential. Remember, the wealth of the cemetery is the potential of the unfinished.

**The wealth of the cemetery
is the potential of the unfinished.**

Potential and the Next Generation

God designed everything not only to reproduce itself but also to transfer and transmit its life and treasure to the next generation. Consider a seed. Every seed comes into this world to deliver a tree, which in turn delivers more seeds, which produce more trees, and on and on it goes. All aspects of creation possess this generational principle.

In the biblical record, God continually stresses the generational principle in all His dealings with man. He instructed Adam and Eve to be fruitful and multiply. He told Abraham that his "seed" would be great and bless the earth. He advised Moses to teach the people to pass on every law and experience to their children and their children's children. He also expressed it through Solomon in the words: "A good man leaves an inheritance to his children's children..." (Proverbs 13:22)

If all the seeds in the world withheld the potential of the trees within them, a natural tragedy would be the result. The bees would suffer, the birds would die, and the animals would starve to death. The genocide of man would also occur as oxygen disappeared from the atmosphere. All this would occur because one element in nature refused to fulfill the purpose for which it was created.

No man is born to live or die unto himself. God gave you the wealth of your potential—your abilities, gifts, talents, energies, creativity, ideas, aspirations and desires—for the blessing of future generations. You bear the responsibility to activate, release and deposit them. This generational principle of God, the Father of creation, is crucial to your full appreciation of the principle of potential. Tragedy strikes whenever a person fails to die empty.

No man is born to live or die unto himself.

I wonder how many hundreds of people—perhaps thousands or millions—were born or are yet to be born who need to benefit from the books you have neglected to write, the songs you have failed to compose, or the invention you have continued to postpone. Perhaps there are millions who need the ministry you have yet to begin or the business venture you have not yet started.

The next generation needs the treasure of your potential. Think of the many inventions, books, songs, works of art and great accomplishments others in past generations have left for you. Even as their treasures have become your blessings, so your treasures must become your children's unborn children's blessings. You must not die unfinished and let the grave steal the gems of the future. Deliver your potential to inspire the children of our world to release theirs.

The next generation needs the treasure of your potential.

A Word to the Third World Mind

History reveals the truth that any people who are robbed by oppression, suppression, depression and subjugation of the opportunity to activate, release and maximize their potential suffer from the loss of generational thinking. Their oppression forces them to think in terms of self-preservation and personal security with little thought for posterity and the future. This mentality pervades many Third World nations today, manifesting itself in an attitude and a lifestyle that encourages *immediate gratification at the expense of the future*. This mindset ultimately leads to fear, distrust, suspicion and resentment among members of the same ethnic community.

This lack of generational consciousness traps individuals in a cycle of self-maintenance and retards creativity, inspiration and innovation. Consequently, the release of the tremendous abilities that lie within every individual is forfeited. Third World people everywhere must be delivered from this mentality. It is essential that they understand the responsibility they have to their children and their children's children. *Until a man can see beyond his own loins, the future is in danger.*

The essence of potential is not preservation but liberation. Although we cannot change the past, we have the potential to chart our destiny and arrange a better future for our children. The opportunity to blame others for the past is often before us; but we can never transfer responsibility for the future to others. You and I have been given by God all that we need to fulfill His purpose for our lives. We possess the ability to impact our homes, our communities, our cities, our nations and perhaps the world if we dare to challenge ourselves and place demands on the vast wealth of potential buried deep within us.

Decide today to do something with your dreams. Disappoint procrastination and commit yourself to releasing your potential. Stop wishing and start willing. Stop proposing and start purposing. Stop procrastinating and start planning. Determine to die empty and leave the earth an inheritance that gives life to others. Remember, few things are impossible to diligence and skill. Great works are performed by perseverance.

PRINCIPLES

1. The fact that you were born is evidence that you possess something that can benefit the world.

2. God gave you potential for the blessing of future generations.

3. The greatest need of ability is responsibility.

4. God places demands on your potential by giving your ability responsibility.

5. Fulfillment is directly related to the successful completion of a task.

6. God has given you everything you need to fulfill His purpose for your life.

Best-sellers from Dr. Myles Munroe

UNDERSTANDING YOUR POTENTIAL helps you to discover your awesome potential. Learn how God has deposited His enormous power within you. Join thousands who have seen the Lord unlock their potential with this book! TPB-168p. ISBN 1-56043-046-X Retail $7.95

WORKBOOK: UNDERSTANDING YOUR POTENTIAL This study guide has been designed to help you better understand and apply the principles discussed in *Understanding Your Potential.* TPB-48p. ISBN 1-56043-092-3 Retail $5.95

Best-sellers from Dr. Myles Munroe

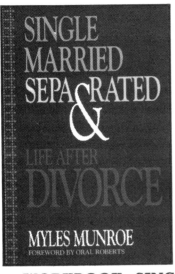

**SINGLE, MARRIED, SEP-
ARATED & LIFE AFTER
DIVORCE** Singleness is a
myth. Marriage is the uniting of
two people for a lifetime.
Separation is an unofficial
divorce. Divorce means to
desert. Read what the Bible
reveals about each. TPB-128p.
ISBN 1-56043-094-X Retail $7.95

**WORKBOOK: SINGLE,
MARRIED, SEPARATED &
LIFE AFTER DIVORCE** This
workbook has been prepared to
help you better understand and
grasp the principles discussed
in *Single, Married, Separated &
Life After Divorce.* TPB-48p.
ISBN 1-56043-115-6 Retail $5.95

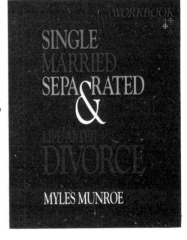

**To order toll free call:
Destiny Image
1-800-722-6774**